SECOND EDITION

face2face

Starter Workbook with Key

Chris Redston with Gillie Cunningham

Contents

Vocabulary, Pronunciation and Spelling	Grammar and Real World	Reading and Writing
Lessons 1A–D p3 **VOCABULARY** numbers 0–12; countries; the alphabet; things in your bag (1); *a* and *an*; people; things; plurals **Pronunciation** word stress (1); /æ/ and /ə/ **Spelling** review	**GRAMMAR** *I, my, you, your; he, his, she, her* **REAL WORLD** saying hello; introducing people; saying goodbye; phone numbers; *Where are you from?*; first names and surnames; classroom language	**Portfolio 1 p52** **Where are you from?** **Reading** three conversations **Writing** full stops (.) and question marks (?); capital letters (1); about you
Lessons 2A–D p8 **VOCABULARY** nationalities; jobs; titles; greetings; numbers 13–100 **Pronunciation** word stress (2); /ɪ/ and /iː/ **Spelling** jobs; plurals	**GRAMMAR** *be* (singular): positive, negative, Wh- questions, yes / no questions and short answers **REAL WORLD** personal information questions; *How old … ?*	**Portfolio 2 p54** **Three people** **Reading** business cards; addresses; forms **Writing** capital letters (2); filling in a form
Lessons 3A–D p13 **VOCABULARY** adjectives (1); word order with adjectives; *very*; family; food and drink (1) and (2); *love, like, eat, drink, a lot of* **Pronunciation** syllables; /ɒ/ and /ʌ/ **Spelling** numbers	**GRAMMAR** *be* (plural): positive, negative, questions and short answers; possessive *'s*; subject pronouns (*I, you*, etc.) and possessive adjectives (*my, your*, etc.) **REAL WORLD** money and prices; *How much … ?*; in a café	**Portfolio 3 p56** **See you soon!** **Reading** holiday emails **Writing** apostrophes; *and* and *but*; a holiday email
Lessons 4A–D p18 **VOCABULARY** phrases with *like, have, live, work, study*; free time activities; things to buy; *this, that, these, those*; days of the week; time words **Pronunciation** syllables and word stress (1) **Spelling** double letters (1)	**GRAMMAR** Present Simple (*I, you, we, they*): positive, negative, questions and short answers **REAL WORLD** in a shop; telling the time; talking about the time	**Portfolio 4 p58** **Internet profiles** **Reading** two internet profiles **Writing** word order (1) and (2); an internet profile
Lessons 5A–D p23 **VOCABULARY** daily routines; time phrases with *on, in, at*; food and drink (3); frequency adverbs and phrases with *every* **Pronunciation** sounds review (1) **Spelling** Present Simple (*he, she, it*)	**GRAMMAR** Present Simple (*he, she, it*): positive, negative, questions and short answers **REAL WORLD** in a restaurant	**Portfolio 5 p60** **My best friend** **Reading** best friends **Writing** *because* and *also*; my best friend
Lessons 6A–D p28 **VOCABULARY** places in a town or city (1) and (2); things in your bag (2); clothes; colours; *favourite* **Pronunciation** /tʃ/ and /dʒ/ **Spelling** silent letters (1)	**GRAMMAR** *a, some, a lot of; there is / there are*: positive, negative, *yes / no* questions and short answers; *any* **REAL WORLD** at the tourist information centre	**Portfolio 6 p62** **A tourist in London** **Reading** a newspaper article **Writing** describing places; places for tourists in your town or city
Lessons 7A–D p33 **VOCABULARY** things you like and don't like; *love, like, don't like, hate*; abilities; prepositions of place; things people do online **Pronunciation** /s/ and /ʃ/ **Spelling** double letters (2); clothes	**GRAMMAR** object pronouns; *can*: positive, negative, *yes / no* questions and short answers **REAL WORLD** asking for and giving directions	**Portfolio 7 p64** **The same or different?** **Reading** people in my family **Writing** sentences with *and, but* and object pronouns; word order (3): *both* and *together*
Answer Key pi–viii		
Lessons 8A–D p38 **VOCABULARY** adjectives (2); years and past time phrases; months and dates; big numbers **Pronunciation** /ɔː/ and /ɜː/ **Spelling** review	**GRAMMAR** Past Simple of *be*: positive, negative, questions and short answers; *was born / were born* **REAL WORLD** talking about days and dates; making suggestions	**Portfolio 8 p66** **Going out** **Reading** entertainment adverts; emails **Writing** *a / an* and *the*; your last film, play or rock concert
Lessons 9A–D p43 **VOCABULARY** transport; holiday activities; at the station; question words **Pronunciation** sounds review (2) **Spelling** silent letters (2)	**GRAMMAR** Past Simple: positive (regular and irregular verbs), negative, questions and short answers **REAL WORLD** buying train tickets; asking about last weekend	**Portfolio 9 p68** **On holiday** **Reading** a travel blog; a holiday in France **Writing** *because, so, when*; your last holiday
Lessons 10A–C p48 **VOCABULARY** future plans; future time phrases; phrases with *have, watch, go, go to*; adjectives (3): feelings **Pronunciation** syllables and word stress (2) **Spelling** Past Simple verb forms	**GRAMMAR** *be going to*: positive, negative, questions and short answers **REAL WORLD** saying goodbye and good luck	**Portfolio 10 p70** **Happy birthday!** **Reading** greetings cards; a thank-you email **Writing** messages on greetings cards; word order: review; a thank-you email
	Starter Reading and Writing Progress Portfolio p72	

1A What's your name?
Language Summary 1, Student's Book p114

Saying hello REAL WORLD 1.1

1 Fill in the gaps with these words or phrases.

| ~~Hello~~ | to meet | my name's |
| You too | What's your | |

PAULA   _Hello_ , I'm Paula. _____ name?
ENZO   Hello, _____ Enzo.
PAULA   Nice _____ you.
ENZO   _____ .

Introducing people REAL WORLD 1.2

2 [S] Write the words.

TIP • [S] = spelling

YVONNE   Robert, t _h_ _i_ _s_ is Meilin.
ROBERT   H ____ , Meilin.
         N ____ to m ____ you.
MEILIN   You t ___ .

Saying goodbye REAL WORLD 1.4

| Hi | thanks | I'm fine | And you | How are |

LENA   _____ , Amir.
AMIR   Hi, Lena. _____ you?
LENA   _____ , thanks.
       _____ ?
AMIR   I'm OK, _____ .

3 [S] Write the words.

LENA   B _y_ _e_ , Amir.
AMIR   G _____ , Lena. S ____ you s ____ .
LENA   Yes, s ____ you.

I, my, you, your GRAMMAR 1.1

4 Fill in the gaps with *I*, *my*, *you* or *your*.

HUGO   Hello, *I* 'm Hugo. What's _____ name?
LIAN   Hi, _____ name's Lian.
HUGO   Nice to meet _____ .
LIAN   _____ too.

CARLA   Hello, Alexei.
ALEXEI   Hi, Carla. How are _____ ?
CARLA   _____ 'm fine, thanks. And _____ ?
ALEXEI   _____ 'm OK, thanks.

Numbers 0–12 VOCABULARY 1.1

5 S Write the numbers.

0 *zero*	5 _____	10 _____
1 _____	6 _____	11 _____
2 _____	7 _____	12 _____
3 _____	8 _____	
4 _____	9 _____	

Phone numbers REAL WORLD 1.3

6 Fill in the gaps with these words.

~~What's~~   number   mobile   It's   your

What's your _____ number?   _____ 07700 900187.

What's _____ home _____ ?   It's 0121 496 0317.

1B Where's she from?

Countries VOCABULARY 1.2

1 S Write the countries.

1 E g y p t

2 I _____

3 A _____

4 the _____

5 B _____

6 S _____

7 C _____

8 G _____

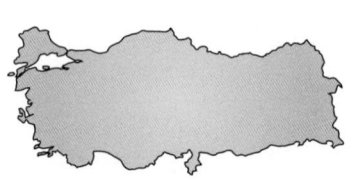
9 T _____

10 the _____

11 M _____

12 R _____

Where are you from? REAL WORLD 1.5

2 Fill in the gaps with these words.

| ~~Hello~~ | And | Where | meet | too | Nice | name's | from | I'm |

FABIEN _Hello_ , I'm Fabien.
CLARA Hi, my _____ Clara.
FABIEN _____ to _____ you.
CLARA You _____ .
FABIEN _____ are you from?
CLARA I'm _____ Spain. _____ you?
FABIEN _____ from France.

Review: introducing people

3 Fill in the gaps with these words.

| ~~Hi~~ | How | Nice | OK | I'm | from | you | this | too | thanks |

EMMA _Hi_ , Brian.
BRIAN Hello, Emma. _____ are you?
EMMA I'm fine, _____ . And _____ ?
BRIAN I'm _____ , thanks.
EMMA Brian, _____ is Kaoru.
BRIAN Hello, Kaoru. _____ to meet you.
KAORU You _____ .
EMMA Where are you _____ ?
KAORU _____ from Osaka, in Japan.

he, his, she, her GRAMMAR 1.2

4 Fill in the gaps with *he*, *his*, *she* or *her*.

¹ _His_ name's Enrique Iglesias.
² _____ 's from Spain.

³ _____ name's Kate Winslet.
⁴ _____ 's from the UK.

A What's ⁵_____ name?
B ⁶_____ name's Will Smith.
A Where's ⁷_____ from?
B ⁸_____ 's from the USA.

A What's ⁹_____ name?
B ¹⁰_____ name's Shakira.
A Where's ¹¹_____ from?
B ¹²_____ 's from Colombia.

1C REAL WORLD > In class

The alphabet VOCABULARY 1.3

1 a Fill in the gaps. Use small letters.

a _b_ c _d_ _ f _ _ i _ _ _ m

n _ _ q r _ _ u _ w _ _ z

b Write the alphabet. Use capital letters.

A B C _____

_____

First names and surnames REAL WORLD 1.6

2 Fill in the gaps with these words.

| spell | ~~your~~ | What's | name | How | surname |

TEACHER What's _your_ first _____, please?
ANTONIO It's Antonio.
TEACHER _____ your _____?
ANTONIO Morales.
TEACHER _____ do you _____ that?
ANTONIO M–o–r–a–l–e–s.

Things in your bag (1) VOCABULARY 1.4
a and an VOCABULARY 1.5

3 S Write the words. Then put *a* or *an* in the boxes.

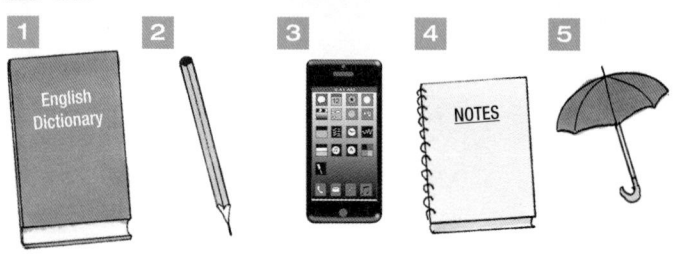
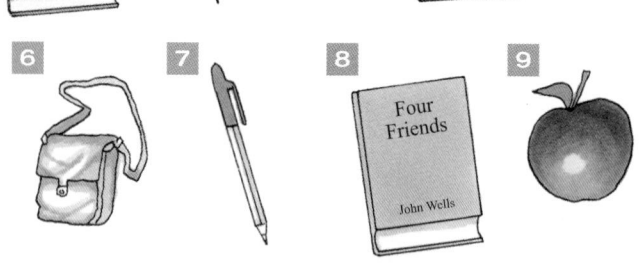

1 _a_ _d i c t i o n a r y_   6 ☐ b _ _ _
2 ☐ p _____   7 ☐ p _ _ _
3 ☐ m _____   8 ☐ b _ _ _
4 ☐ n _____   9 ☐ a _ _ _
5 ☐ u _____

Classroom language REAL WORLD 1.7

4 Fill in the gaps with these phrases.

| ~~Excuse me~~   in English   What does |
| I don't know   I don't understand |
| Can you repeat that   How do you spell |

GABRIELA [1] _Excuse me_ .
TEACHER   Yes, Gabriela?
GABRIELA [2] _____ dictionary?
TEACHER   D–i–c–t–i–o–n–a–r–y.
GABRIELA Thank you.

JOHANN   Excuse me. [3] _____
          surname mean?
TEACHER   It's your family name.
JOHANN   I'm sorry, [4] _____ .
TEACHER   Your first name is Johann. Your surname
          is Schulz.
JOHANN   Oh, OK. Thank you.

TEACHER   Look at the photo on page 12.
YOUSSEF   [5] _____ , please?
TEACHER   Look at the photo on page 12.

DENIZ   Excuse me. What's this
          [6] _____ ?
TEACHER   It's a notebook.
DENIZ   OK, thank you.

TEACHER   Jiang, what's the answer to question 2?
JIANG   I'm sorry, [7] _____ .

VOCABULARY AND SKILLS 1D — People and things

People VOCABULARY 1.6   Things VOCABULARY 1.7

1 S Do the crossword.

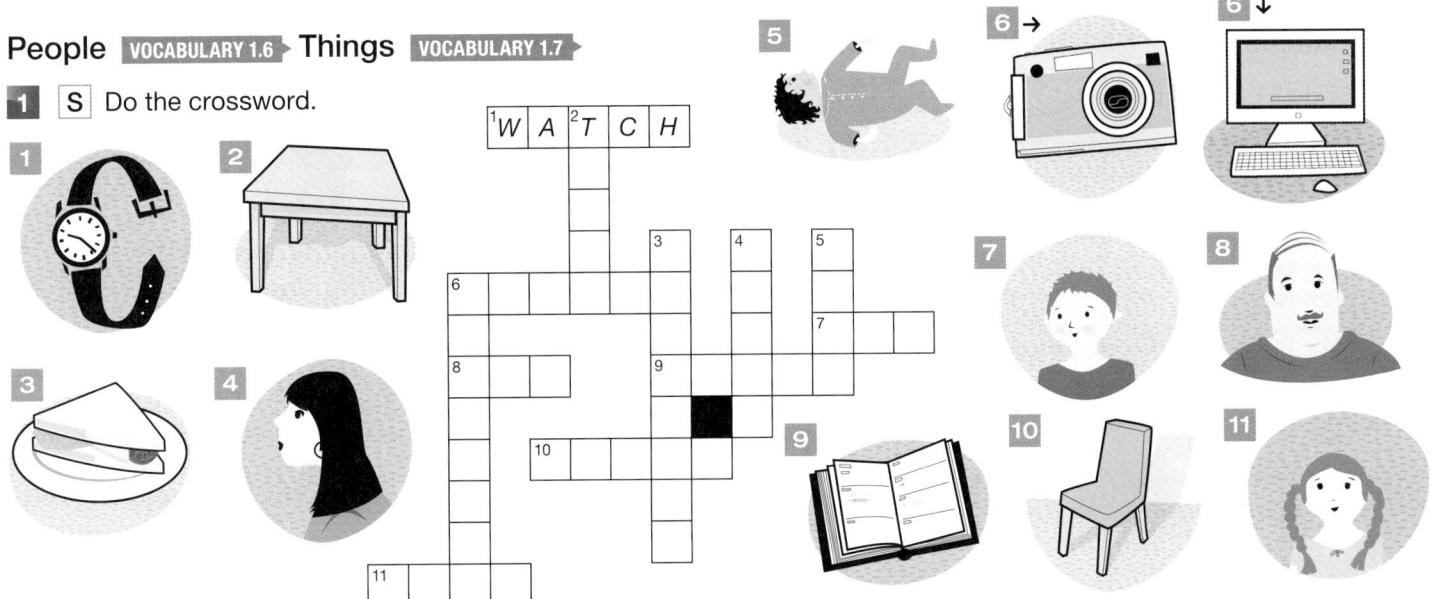

Plurals VOCABULARY 1.8

2 Write the plurals.

1 a student — students
2 a teacher
3 a person
4 a thing
5 a baby
6 a man
7 a name
8 a country
9 a sandwich
10 a woman
11 a watch
12 an answer

Pronunciation: word stress (1)

3 Mark the stress (ˈ) on these words.

1 Italy   7 computer
2 Brazil   8 notebook
3 Russia   9 dictionary
4 Germany   10 umbrella
5 Australia   11 apple
6 Turkey   12 mobile

Pronunciation: /æ/ and /ə/

HELP WITH PRONUNCIATION Student's Book p13

4 Look at the letters in **bold**. Match the words to the sounds.

m**a**n   t**ea**ch**er**   **a**pple   pr**a**ctise   voc**a**bulary
Chin**a**   wom**a**n   s**a**ndwich   Br**a**zil   It**a**ly

/æ/	/ə/
bag	computer
man	teacher

Spelling: review

5 S Circle the words with the correct spelling.

1 Brasil / (Brazil)   6 notbook / notebook
2 eihgt / eight   7 sorry / sory
3 pencil / pensil   8 sanwich / sandwich
4 umbrela / umbrella   9 sirname / surname
5 phone / fone   10 first name / furst name

Reading and Writing Portfolio 1 p52

2A She's British

Language Summary 2, Student's Book p116

Nationalities VOCABULARY 2.1

1 Find 15 nationalities (→↓).

```
A C I T A L I A N D S R
G H B U F O F U Z S Z U
E I O R D X R S Q P B S
R N N K A D E T O A R S
M E X I C A N R P N A I
A S V S Y M C A H I Z A
N E U H I T H L E S I N
J U L B R I T I S H L K
B E G Y P T I A N X I E
A M E R I C A N D C A W
W E C O L O M B I A N A
J A P A N E S E A Q U L
```

be (singular): positive GRAMMAR 2.1

2 Fill in gaps 1–11 with 'm, 're or 's.

His name¹ **'s** Roger.
He² ___ from the USA.
Her name³ ___ Camille.
She⁴ ___ French.

Hello, I⁵ ___ Alicia.
I⁶ ___ Colombian.

You⁷ ___ in the Starter class.

Hello, my name⁸ ___ Hiro.
I⁹ ___ Japanese and
I¹⁰ ___ a manager.

This is my car.
It¹¹ ___ Italian.

be (singular): negative GRAMMAR 2.2

3 Make these sentences negative.

1 I'm a teacher.
   I'm not a teacher.

2 He's a student.
   _____

3 You're from Russia.
   _____

4 It's German.
   _____

5 She's Chinese.
   _____

6 I'm British.
   _____

7 My teacher's American.
   _____

8 You're a singer.
   _____

4 Tick (✓) the true sentences. Make the other sentences negative. Write the correct sentences.

1 New Delhi is the capital of India. ✓
2 Kylie Minogue is British.
   Kylie Minogue isn't British. She's Australian.
3 Cameron Diaz is from Spain.

4 Renault is a French company.

5 Big Ben is in Washington.

6 Daniel Craig is Russian.

7 Starbucks is a British company.

8 Tokyo is the capital of Japan.

2B What's your job?

Jobs VOCABULARY 2.2

1 S Write the jobs.

a m*a n a g e r*

an a _ _ _ _ _ _ _ _

an a _ _ _ _ _ _

a t _ _ _ _ d _ _ _ _ _

a s _ _ _ _ _ _
a _ _ _ _ _ _ _ _ _

a m _ _ _ _ _ _ _

a p _ _ _ _ _ _
o _ _ _ _ _ _ _

a w _ _ _ _ _ _ _

a w _ _ _ _ _

a d _ _ _ _ _

a t _ _ _ _ _ _ _

be (singular): *Wh-* questions GRAMMAR 2.3

2 Fill in the gaps in these conversations.

Conversation 1

A Hello, _what's_ your name?
B _____ name's Oliver.
A Where _____ you from?
B _____ from the UK.
A _____ your job?
B _____ an actor.

Conversation 2

A Hi, _____ your name?
B My _____ Holly.
A _____ are you _____ ?
B _____ _____ the USA.
A _____ _____ job?
B _____ actress.

3 Look at photos 1–4. Fill in the gaps in the conversations.

Bruce

A _What's_ his name?
B His _____ Bruce.
A _____ he from?
B _____ from Australia.
A _____ his job?
B _____ a waiter.

Aylin

A _____ her name?
B _____ _____ Aylin.
A _____ _____ from?
B _____ from Turkey.
A _____ _____ job?
B _____ a doctor.

Hamadi

A _____ _____ name?
B _____ _____ Hamadi.
A _____ _____ from?
B _____ _____ Egypt.
A _____ _____ job?
B _____ _____ manager.

Carolina

A _____ _____ _____ ?
B _____ _____ Carolina.
A _____ _____ _____ ?
B _____ _____ Mexico.
A _____ _____ _____ ?
B _____ _____ teacher.

be (singular): *yes / no* questions and short answers GRAMMAR 2.4

4 a Make questions with these words.

1 Australia / from / Is / Bruce ?
   Is Bruce from Australia?
2 police officer / he / Is / a ?
   _____
3 Aylin / Is / Germany / from ?
   _____
4 she / Is / doctor / a ?
   _____
5 France / from / Is / Hamadi ?
   _____
6 he / Is / manager / a ?
   _____
7 from / Is / Mexico / Carolina ?
   _____
8 waitress / she / Is / a ?
   _____

b Write short answers to the questions in **4a**.

1 _Yes, he is._
2 _____
3 _____
4 _____
5 _____
6 _____
7 _____
8 _____

5 Fill in the gaps with *am*, *'m*, *are*, *is* or *isn't*.

1 A _Am_ I in this class?
   B Yes, you _____ .
2 A _____ you Russian?
   B Yes, I _____ .
3 A _____ your car Japanese?
   B No, it _____ .
4 A _____ you a musician?
   B No, I _____ not.
5 A _____ this your bag?
   B Yes, it _____ .

2C REAL WORLD — Personal information

Titles VOCABULARY 2.3 › Greetings VOCABULARY 2.4

1 Complete the conversations with these titles and greetings.

> Mr   Mrs   Good evening (x2)
> Good morning (x2)   Good night (x2)
> Good afternoon (x2)

1 _____ , Janet.

2 _____ , Clive.

3 _____ , Sophie.

4 _____ , Mum.

5 _____ , 6 _____ Jones.

7 _____ .

8 _____ , 9 _____ Clark.

10 _____ .

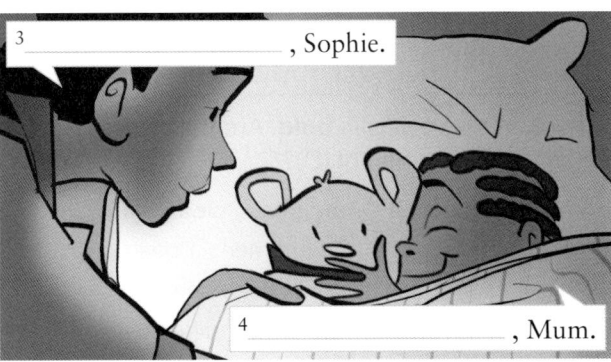

Personal information questions REAL WORLD 2.2

2 Read the conversation. Fill in the gaps with these questions.

> ~~What's your first name, please?~~   What's your nationality?
> How do you spell that?   Can you repeat that, please?
> What's your surname?   What's your email address?
> What's your address?   What's your mobile number?

ELLEN Good afternoon. Please take a seat.
NEIL Thank you.
ELLEN Welcome to the BRSC Bank. My name's Ellen.
NEIL Nice to meet you.
ELLEN You too. [1] *What's your first name, please?*
NEIL It's Neil.
ELLEN Thank you. [2] _____
NEIL It's Horton.
ELLEN [3] _____
NEIL H–o–r–t–o–n.
ELLEN Thank you. [4] _____
NEIL I'm Australian.
ELLEN [5] _____
NEIL It's 17 William Street, London SE18 4ED.
ELLEN [6] _____
NEIL Yes, it's 17 William Street, London SE18 4ED.
ELLEN Thanks. [7] _____
NEIL It's neil.horton@webmail.co.uk.
ELLEN OK. [8] _____
NEIL It's 07700 900769.
ELLEN Thank you very much.

VOCABULARY 2D AND SKILLS — How old is she?

Numbers 13–100 VOCABULARY 2.5

1 S Write the numbers and mark the stress (˚).

a 13 thírteen
b 30 t_____
c 14 f_____
d 40 f_____
e 15 f_____
f 50 f_____
g 16 s_____
h 60 s_____
i 17 s_____
j 70 s_____
k 18 e_____
l 80 e_____
m 19 n_____
n 90 n_____

2 Write the answers in words.

a eighty-six – twenty-two = _sixty-four_
b thirty-one + forty-six = _____
c eighty-nine – sixty-three = _____
d twenty-four + eighteen = _____
e ninety-three – forty-two = _____
f sixty-six + thirty-four = _____

How old … ? REAL WORLD 2.3

3 Fill in the gaps with these words and phrases.

| How old | How old is | How old are |
| I'm | He's | years |

1_____ is your car?
It's eighty-one 2_____ old.

This is Max.
Hello. 3_____ you?
4_____ seven.

5_____ your dog?
6_____ twelve.

Pronunciation: word stress (2)

4 Mark the stress (˚) on these nationalities.

1 German
2 Russian
3 American
4 British
5 Chinese
6 Spanish
7 Brazilian
8 Italian
9 Turkish
10 Australian

Pronunciation: /ɪ/ and /iː/

HELP WITH PRONUNCIATION Student's Book p21

5 a Look at these pictures. Check you remember the sounds /ɪ/ and /iː/.

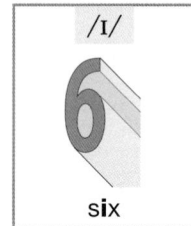 six

 nineteen

b Look at the vowels in **bold**. Are the vowel sounds the same (S) or different (D)?

1 s**i**x n**i**net**ee**n D
2 th**i**ng s**i**ngle S
3 h**e**'s h**i**s
4 **e**mail Chin**e**se
5 watch**e**s p**eo**ple
6 M**i**ss pl**ea**se
7 w**o**men Br**i**tish
8 p**o**lice sh**e**'s
9 f**i**fteen fift**ee**n
10 **e**vening **e**vening

Spelling: jobs

6 S Write the vowels (a, e, i, o, u) in these jobs.

1 a t_e_ a ch_e_r
2 a w__t__r
3 a w__tr__ss
4 a d__ct__r
5 an __ct__r
6 an __ctr__ss
7 a t__x__ dr__v__r
8 a m__n__g__r

Spelling: plurals

7 S Circle the correct plurals.

1 (chairs) / chaires
2 diarys / diaries
3 girls / girles
4 watchs / watches
5 countrys / countries
6 sandwiches / sandwichs
7 babies / babys
8 mans / men
9 women / wimin
10 poeple / people

Reading and Writing Portfolio 2 p54

3A Two cities

Language Summary 3, Student's Book p118

Adjectives (1) VOCABULARY 3.1

1 a [S] Write the vowels (*a, e, i, o, u*) in these adjectives.

1 b a d
2 h _ t
3 n _ w
4 sm _ ll
5 fr _ _ ndly
6 b _ _ _ t _ f _ l
7 _ xp _ ns _ v _

b [S] Write the opposites of the adjectives in **1a**.

1 good
2 _____
3 _____
4 _____
5 _____
6 _____
7 _____

Word order with adjectives; *very*
VOCABULARY 3.2

2 Make sentences with these words.

1 Her / beautiful / very / is / cat .
   Her cat is very beautiful.

2 friendly / My / is / teacher / very .

3 It's / phone / a / old / very .

4 a / She's / doctor / good .

5 bags / are / The / expensive .

6 very / a / It's / house / big .

7 is / country / hot / a / Egypt .

8 are / The / nice / sandwiches / very .

9 dictionary / good / very / is / His .

be (plural): positive and negative GRAMMAR 3.1

3 Read the email. Fill in the gaps with the correct positive (+) or negative (–) form of *be*.

Hi Charlotte
How ¹ *are* (+) you? We² _____ (+) in Thailand! It³ _____ (+) a beautiful country and the people ⁴ _____ (+) very friendly. We ⁵ _____ (–) in Bangkok, we⁶ _____ (+) in a nice hotel in Chiang Mai. The hotel ⁷ _____ (–) expensive and the manager⁸ _____ (+) very friendly. The rooms ⁹ _____ (–) very big, but they¹⁰ _____ (+) very nice. Derek ¹¹ _____ (–) in the hotel now, he¹² _____ (+) in a café. And it¹³ _____ (+) very hot here! See you soon.
Love Molly and Derek
PS Here's a photo of our new friends!

be (plural): questions and short answers GRAMMAR 3.2

4 a Fill in the gaps with *is*, *'s* or *are*.

1 Where *are* Molly and Derek?
2 _____ the people very friendly?
3 _____ Molly and Derek in Bangkok?
4 Where _____ the hotel?
5 _____ the hotel expensive?
6 _____ the rooms very big?
7 Where _____ Derek now?
8 _____ it very hot in Thailand?

b Write the answers to the questions in **4a**.

1 *They're in Thailand.*
2 _____
3 _____
4 _____
5 _____
6 _____
7 _____
8 _____

Review: contractions (1)

5 Write these sentences with contractions (*I'm*, *he's*, *aren't*, etc.).

1. He is from New York.
   He's from New York.
2. I am from Moscow.
3. You are not in this class.
4. He is not from London.
5. What is your name?
6. She is not Spanish, she is Mexican.
7. We are in Poland and it is very cold.
8. They are not actors, they are waiters.

Review: short answers

6 Choose the correct short answers (a, b or c).

1. Are we in room 23?
   (a) Yes, we are.   b Yes, I am.   c Yes, we're.
2. Are you cold?
   a No, I isn't.   b No, I not.   c No, I'm not.
3. Is Hannah from Germany?
   a Yes, she's.   b Yes, she is.   c Yes, she's is.
4. Are your friends at the hotel?
   a No, they not.   b No, they isn't.   c No, they aren't.
5. Am I in your class?
   a Yes, you are.   b Yes, are you.   c Yes, you're.
6. Is Bruno a good musician?
   a No, he not.   b No, he isn't.   c No, he aren't.
7. Is your city very beautiful?
   a Yes, it's.   b Yes, is it.   c Yes, it is.
8. Are you and Francesca at school now?
   a No, we aren't.   b No, aren't we.   c No, we not.

3B Brothers and sisters

Family VOCABULARY 3.3

1 Look at the Clark family. Fill in the gaps with these words.

| ~~father~~ | mother | husband | wife | son |
| daughter | brother | sister | children | parents |

1. Frank is Paul's *father* .
2. Paul is Frank's _____ .
3. Frank is Daisy's _____ .
4. Jane is Daisy's _____ .
5. Daisy is Frank's _____ .
6. Jane is Paul's _____ .
7. Daisy is Paul's _____ .
8. Paul is Millie's _____ .
9. Frank and Daisy are Paul, Jane and Millie's _____ .
10. Paul, Jane and Millie are Frank and Daisy's _____ .

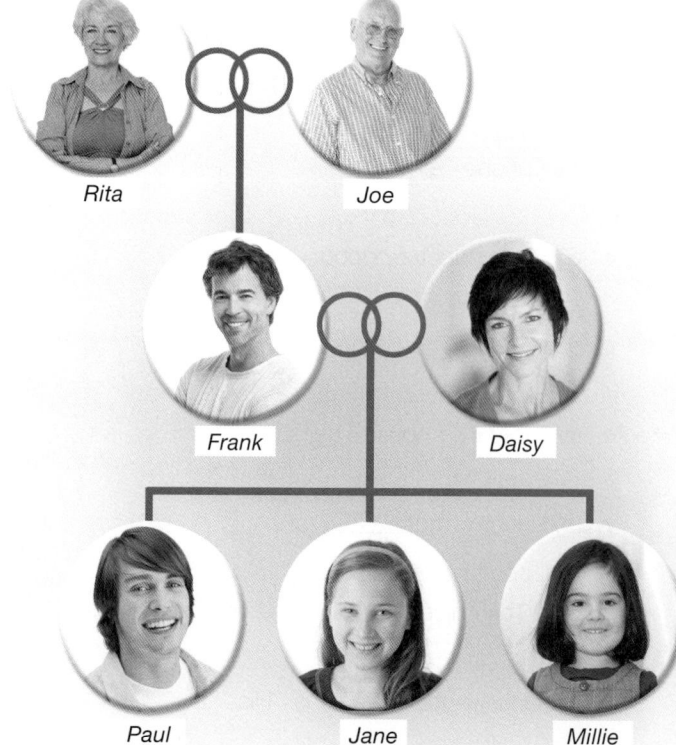

Rita   *Joe*
Frank   *Daisy*
Paul   *Jane*   *Millie*

2 Look again at the Clark family. Fill in the gaps with these words.

> ~~grandparents~~   grandchildren   grandfather
> grandmother   grandson   granddaughter

1 Rita and Joe are Paul's _grandparents_ .
2 Jane is Rita's _____ .
3 Rita is Jane's _____ .
4 Paul is Joe's _____ .
5 Joe is Millie's _____ .
6 Paul, Jane and Millie are Rita and Joe's _____ .

Possessive 's GRAMMAR 3.3

3 Fill in the gaps with the correct names and 's.

1 Paul is Jane and _Millie's_ brother.
2 Rita is _____ mother.
3 Joe is _____ husband.
4 Rita is _____ wife.
5 Joe is _____ father.
6 Frank is Joe and _____ son.
7 Jane is Frank and _____ daughter.
8 Millie is Paul and _____ sister.

4 Write *is* or *P* (= the possessive) for 's in these sentences.

1 She**'s** a doctor.   's = _is_
2 Nigel is Steve**'s** brother. 's = _P_
3 His name**'s** Brett.   's = ____
4 Bianca**'s** an actress.   's = ____
5 Gary**'s** wife is French.   's = ____
6 Vicky**'s** parents are Italian. 's = ____
7 My teacher**'s** from the UK. 's = ____
8 My teacher**'s** name is Ed.   's = ____

Subject pronouns (*I, you*, etc.) and possessive adjectives (*my, your*, etc.) GRAMMAR 3.4

5 Fill in the gaps in the table.

subject pronouns	I	____	he	she	____	we	they
possessive adjectives	my	your	____	____	its	____	____

6 Choose the correct words.

1 Where's *I* / (*my*) dictionary?
2 Kathy and Penny are *we* / *our* children.
3 What's *he* / *his* mother's name?
4 *We* / *Our* aren't from the USA.
5 Is Justin *you* / *your* brother?
6 *I* / *My* friend Ray is *she* / *her* father.
7 *It* / *Its* isn't very expensive.
8 What's *they* / *their* surname?
9 *They* / *Their* aren't *he* / *his* parents.
10 Is *she* / *her* in *you* / *your* class?

Review: *be*

7 Fill in the gaps with the correct form of *be*.

ROSE This ¹ _is_ a photo of my grandchildren.
HILDA How old ² _____ they?
ROSE Cassie³ _____ twenty-one and Noah⁴ _____ nineteen.
HILDA ⁵ _____ they students?
ROSE No, they ⁶ _____ . Cassie⁷ _____ an actress and Noah⁸ _____ a waiter.

MUM Hello, Erin. ⁹ _____ you OK?
ERIN Yes, I¹⁰ _____ fine, Mum.
MUM Where ¹¹ _____ you?
ERIN I¹² _____ with Silvia. We¹³ _____ in a café.
MUM ¹⁴ _____ Olivia with you?
ERIN No, she ¹⁵ _____ . She¹⁶ _____ at a friend's house.

3C REAL WORLD: Eat in or take away?

Food and drink (1) VOCABULARY 3.4

1 S Write the letters in these words for food and drink.

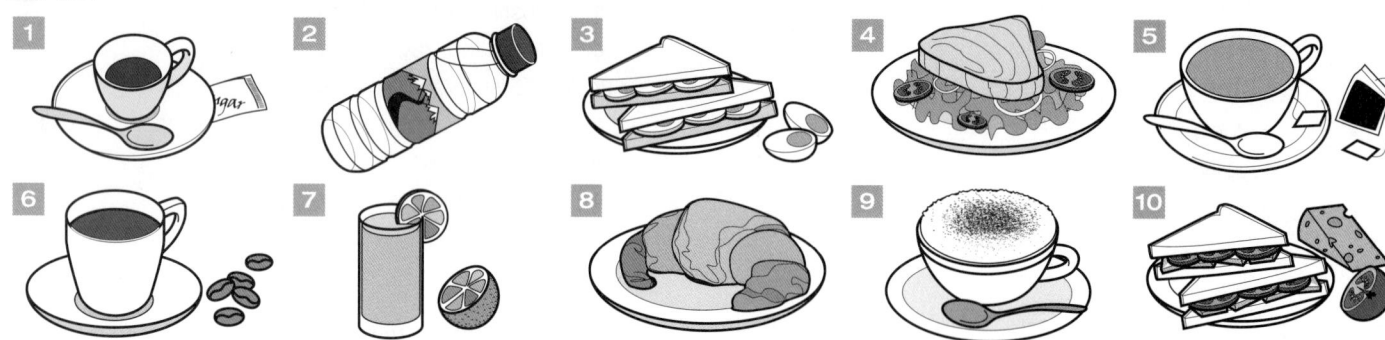

1 an e _s_ p _r_ e _s s_ o
2 a m _i_ n _e_ r _a_ l w _a t e_ r
3 an e _gg_ s _an_ dw _ic_ h
4 a t _un_ a s _a l a_ d
5 a t _ea_
6 a c _o f f e e_
7 an o _ra_ ng _e_ j _ui_ c _e_
8 a c _r_ ois _s_ a _n_ t
9 a c _a_ pp _u_ cc _i_ n _o_
10 a ch _ee_ s _e_ and t _o m a t_ o s _an_ dw _ic_ h

Money and prices REAL WORLD 3.1

2 Write these prices in words.

a $75 — seventy-five dollars
b €7 _____
c 20c _____
d £15 _____
e 25p _____
f £9.70 _____

How much ... ? REAL WORLD 3.2

3 Fill in the gaps with *How much is* or *How much are*.

A ¹_____ the small bag?
B It's £39.99.

A ²_____ these pens?
B They're £2.95.

A ³_____ the croissants?
B They're €1.60.

A ⁴_____ this watch?
B It's $100.

In a café REAL WORLD 3.3

4 Read these conversations. Fill in the gaps with these words.

| ~~Can~~ | that's | away | in | welcome |
| Thanks | Anything | please | Eat | |

ASSISTANT   _Can_ I help you?
CUSTOMER 1   Yes, a coffee and a croissant, _____.
ASSISTANT   Sure. _____ else?
CUSTOMER 1   No, that's all, thanks.
ASSISTANT   Eat _____ or take _____?
CUSTOMER 1   _____ in, please.
ASSISTANT   OK, _____ £3.50, please.
CUSTOMER 1   _____ a lot.
ASSISTANT   You're _____.

| away | help | else | Sure | You're |
| Thank | take | Eat | much | please |

ASSISTANT   Can I _____ you?
CUSTOMER 2   Yes, a cappuccino, please.
ASSISTANT   _____. Anything _____?
CUSTOMER 2   Yes, an egg sandwich, _____.
ASSISTANT   _____ in or _____ away?
CUSTOMER 2   Take _____, please.
ASSISTANT   OK, that's £4.75, please.
CUSTOMER 2   _____ you very _____.
ASSISTANT   _____ welcome.

VOCABULARY 3D AND SKILLS: Food I like

Food and drink (2) VOCABULARY 3.5

1 S Do the crossword.

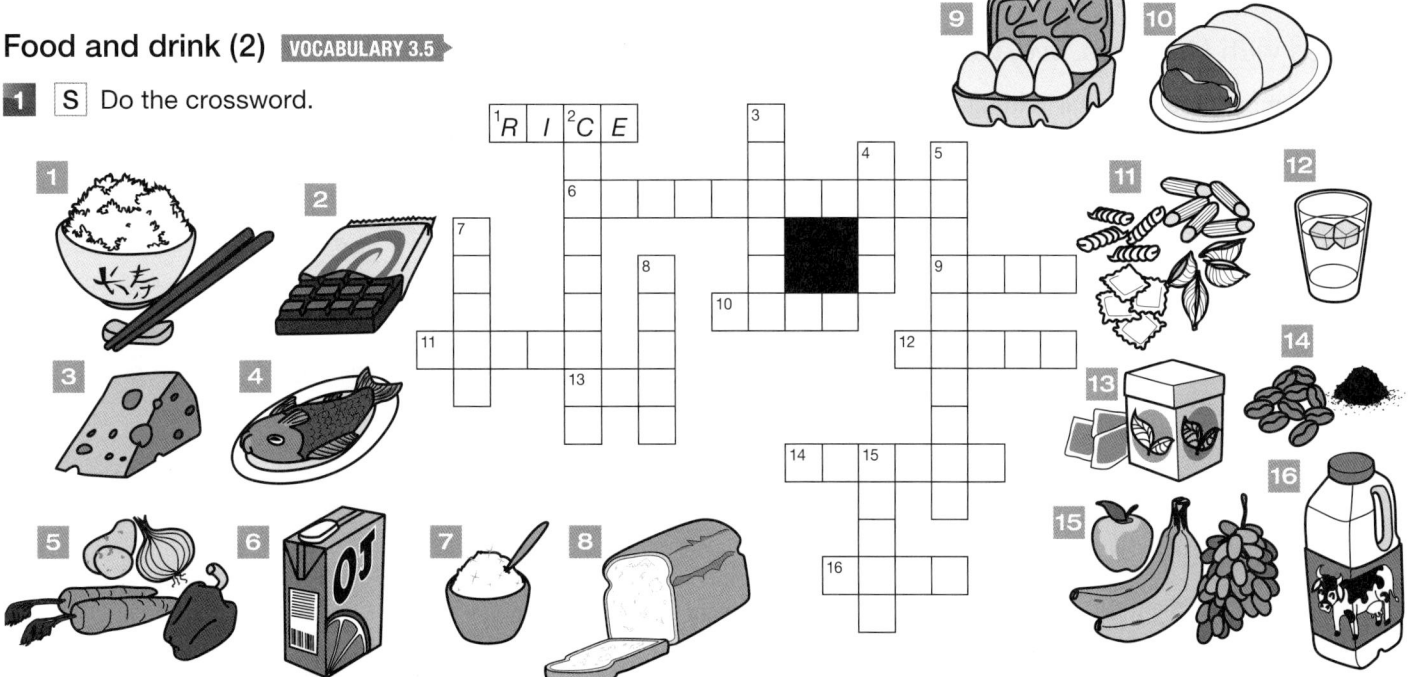

love, like, eat, drink, a lot of
VOCABULARY 3.6

2 a Complete the words.

1 I l__ k__ fish and rice.
2 I d_____ a l____ of milk.
3 I e___ a l____ of vegetables.
4 I l__ v__ chocolate.

b Tick (✓) the sentences in **2a** that are true for you.

Pronunciation: syllables

3 a Look at these words. Notice the number of syllables.

big = 1 syllable
British = 2 syllables (Brit–ish)
computer = 3 syllables (com–pu–ter)

b Write the number of syllables in these words.

a friendly   _2_   f beautiful   ___
b unfriendly ___   g husband   ___
c cheap   ___   h wife   ___
d expensive   ___   i grandson   ___
e ugly   ___   j grandchildren ___

Pronunciation: /ɒ/ and /ʌ/

HELP WITH PRONUNCIATION
Student's Book p29

4 a Look at these pictures. Check you remember the sounds /ɒ/ and /ʌ/.

 /ɒ/ coffee

 /ʌ/ umbrella

b Look at the vowels in **bold**. Circle the correct vowel sounds.

1 **o**range   (/ɒ/) /ʌ/   6 m**o**ther   /ɒ/ /ʌ/
2 br**o**ther   /ɒ/ (/ʌ/)   7 d**o**llar   /ɒ/ /ʌ/
3 h**u**sband   /ɒ/ /ʌ/   8 w**a**tch   /ɒ/ /ʌ/
4 ch**o**colate /ɒ/ /ʌ/   9 l**o**ve   /ɒ/ /ʌ/
5 d**o**ctor   /ɒ/ /ʌ/   10 s**o**n   /ɒ/ /ʌ/

Spelling: numbers

5 S Write these numbers in words.

a 5   _five_   g 99 _____
b 15 _____   h 11 _____
c 56 _____   i 12 _____
d 14 _____   j 83 _____
e 40 _____   k 31 _____
f 28 _____   l 100 _____

Reading and Writing Portfolio 3 p56

17

4A Live, work and study
Language Summary 4, Student's Book p120

Phrases with *like, have, live, work, study* VOCABULARY 4.1

1 Look at pictures 1–10. Fill in the gaps with these words.

~~study~~	have	football	work	children
live	centre	like	car	languages	city
British	music	office	flat	company

study English

_____ in an _____

like _____

_____ in a _____

study _____

_____ rock _____

have a _____

live in the _____ of the _____

_____ two _____

work for a _____

Present Simple (I, you, we, they): positive and negative

GRAMMAR 4.1

2 Read about Josef. Fill in the gaps with the positive (+) or negative (–) of *like, have, live, work* or *study*.

My name's Josef and I ¹ _live_ (+) in Berlin, in Germany. I'm married and my wife's name is Claudia. We ² _____ (+) two daughters, Katia and Elise, but we ³ _____ (–) a son. Katia is 12 and Elise is 15. They ⁴ _____ (+) languages at school and their English is very good. They ⁵ _____ (+) rock music and Italian food, but they ⁶ _____ (–) Chinese food.
We ⁷ _____ (+) in a very nice flat in the centre of the city. I'm a teacher and I ⁸ _____ (+) in a school near our flat. We ⁹ _____ (–) a dog, but we ¹⁰ _____ (+) three cats.

Josef

3 a Choose the correct verbs.

1 *work* / (*study*) Italian
2 *like* / *live* Japanese food
3 *have* / *study* a new computer
4 *like* / *live* in an old house
5 *work* / *study* Spanish
6 *live* / *have* in the USA
7 *live* / *have* a good camera
8 *like* / *work* in a café
9 *like* / *live* chocolate

b Write eight sentences about you. Use the phrases in **3a** and the Present Simple positive or negative.

1 _I don't study Italian._
2 _____
3 _____
4 _____
5 _____
6 _____
7 _____
8 _____
9 _____

4B   My free time

Free time activities   VOCABULARY 4.2

1 a **S** Write the missing letters in these phrases.

watch T *V* or D *V D* s

play t _ _ _ _ s

go o _ _ with f _ _ _ _ _ _ s

play v _ _ _ _ o g _ _ _ _ s

go to the c _ _ _ _ _ a

eat o _ _

go to c _ _ _ _ _ _ s

go s _ _ _ _ _ _ g

b Tick (✓) the things in **1a** you do in your free time.

Present Simple (*I, you, we, they*): questions and short answers GRAMMAR 4.2

2 Read about the American rock band Midnight. Fill in the gaps with these verbs.

| ~~like~~ | watch | have | play |
| live | drink | love | eat (x2) |

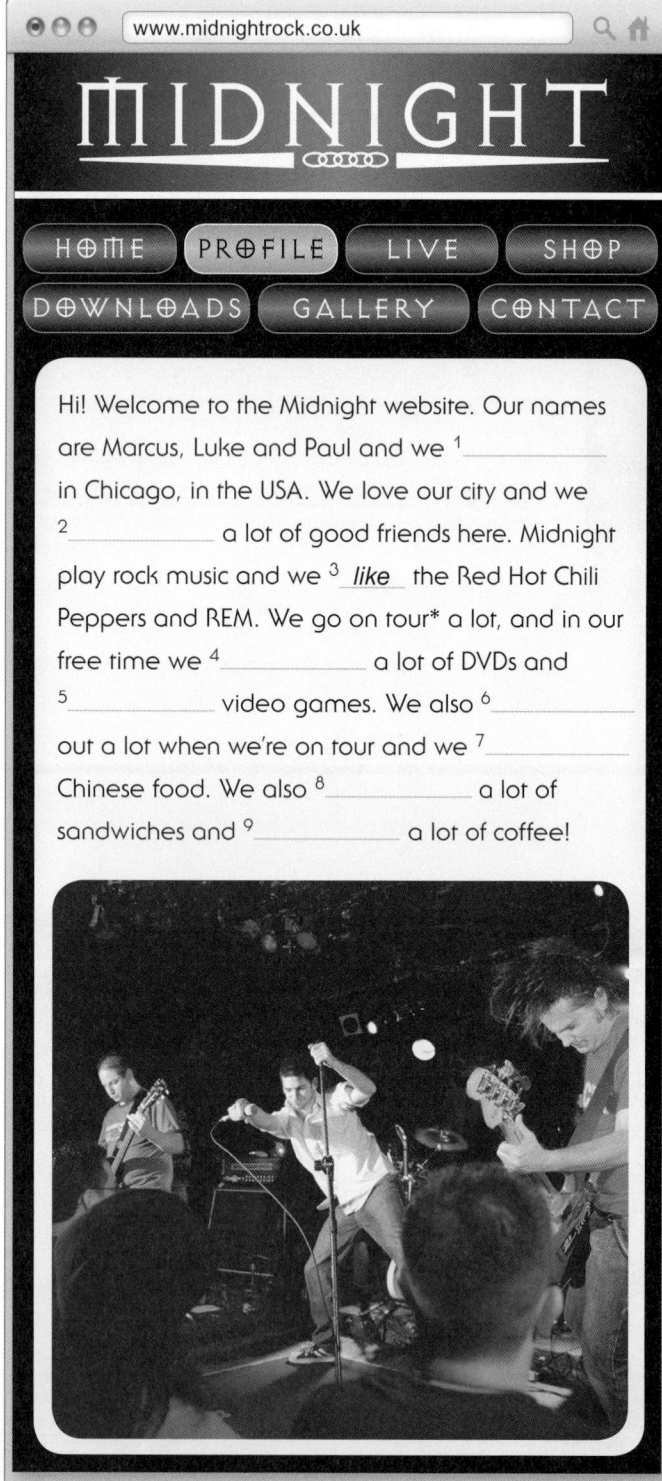

www.midnightrock.co.uk

MIDNIGHT

HOME PROFILE LIVE SHOP
DOWNLOADS GALLERY CONTACT

Hi! Welcome to the Midnight website. Our names are Marcus, Luke and Paul and we ¹_____ in Chicago, in the USA. We love our city and we ²_____ a lot of good friends here. Midnight play rock music and we ³ _like_ the Red Hot Chili Peppers and REM. We go on tour* a lot, and in our free time we ⁴_____ a lot of DVDs and ⁵_____ video games. We also ⁶_____ out a lot when we're on tour and we ⁷_____ Chinese food. We also ⁸_____ a lot of sandwiches and ⁹_____ a lot of coffee!

*go on tour = go from city to city and play concerts

3 Read about Midnight again. Then fill in the gaps in these questions.

1 A Where _do_ Marcus, Luke and Paul _live_ ?
  B In Chicago, in the USA.
2 A _____ they like Chicago?
  B Yes, they do.
3 A What music _____ they _____ ?
  B They like the Red Hot Chili Peppers and REM.
4 A _____ _____ they _____ in their free time?
  B They watch DVDs and play video games.
5 A _____ _____ eat _____ a lot?
  B Yes, they do.
6 A _____ food _____ they like?
  B Chinese food.
7 A _____ _____ a lot of sandwiches?
  B Yes, they do.
8 A _____ _____ a lot of coffee?
  B Yes, they do.

4 Make questions with these words. Then write the short answers.

1 write / I / the questions / Do ?
  Do I write the questions?
  (✓) Yes, _you do._
2 I / you / know / Do ?
  _____
  (✗) No, _____
3 office / you / in / Do / work / an ?
  _____
  (✓) _____
4 Do / big / you / a / have / flat ?
  _____
  (✗) _____
5 a / today / we / class / have / Do ?
  _____
  (✓) _____
6 Pete and Andy / football / like / Do ?
  _____
  (✓) _____
7 parents / Do / car / your / a / have ?
  _____
  (✗) _____

4C REAL WORLD Buying things

Things to buy VOCABULARY 4.3

1 S Do the puzzle. Find the thing to buy (↓).

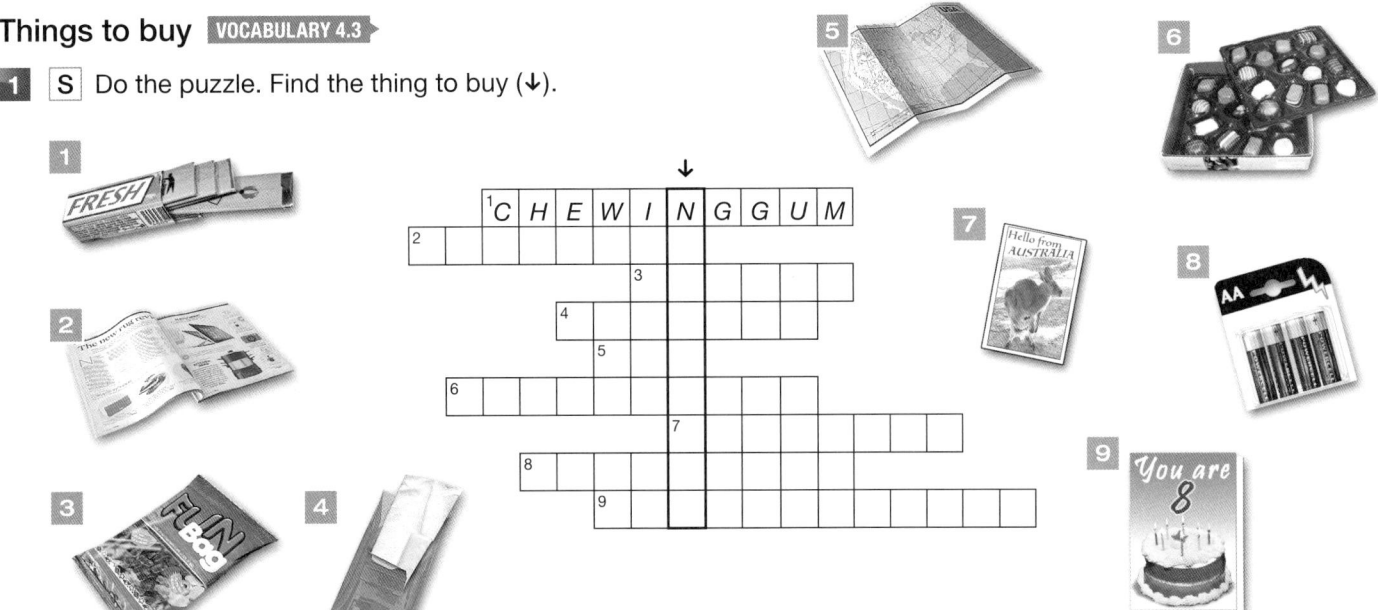

this, that, these, those VOCABULARY 4.4

2 Fill in the gaps with *this*, *that*, *these* or *those*.

Who are ¹ _those_ people?

² _____'s my sister and ³ _____ are her children.

How much are ⁴ _____ watches?

They're £19.99.

Excuse me. Is ⁵ _____ Mr Brown's office?

No, ⁶ _____'s his office over there.

In a shop REAL WORLD 4.1

3 a Read this conversation in a shop. Fill in the gaps with these phrases.

| ~~Excuse me~~ | Goodbye | can I have | No, that's all |
| How much are | Do you have | Here you are | |

CUSTOMER ¹ _Excuse me_ . ² _____ any AA batteries?

ASSISTANT Yes, they're over there, near the birthday cards.

CUSTOMER Thanks. ³ _____ they?

ASSISTANT They're £3.99 for four.

CUSTOMER OK. And ⁴ _____ that small box of chocolates, please?

ASSISTANT Sure. Anything else?

CUSTOMER ⁵ _____ , thanks.

ASSISTANT OK. That's £8.49, please.

CUSTOMER ⁶ _____ .

ASSISTANT Thanks a lot. Bye.

CUSTOMER ⁷ _____ .

b Read the conversation again. How much is the box of chocolates?

£ _____

4D VOCABULARY AND SKILLS

What time is it?

Days of the week VOCABULARY 4.5

1 S Write the days of the week.

1 M o n d a y
2 T _ _ _ _ _ _
3 W _ _ _ _ _ _ _ _
4 T _ _ _ _ _ _ _
5 F _ _ _ _ _
6 S _ _ _ _ _ _
7 S _ _ _ _ _

Time words VOCABULARY 4.6

2 Fill in the gaps with these words.

| ~~seconds~~ | year | days | months |
| weeks | hour | minutes | |

a three hundred *seconds*
   = five _____

b thirty minutes = half an _____

c forty-eight hours = two _____

d twenty-one days = three _____

e fifty-two weeks = one _____

f one year = twelve _____

Telling the time REAL WORLD 4.2

3 Write these times in two ways.

1 *eight o'clock*
   eight

2 _____
   _____

3 _____
   _____

4 _____
   _____

4 Write these times with *past* or *to*.

1 *ten past nine*
2 _____
3 _____
4 _____
5 _____
6 _____
7 _____
8 _____

Talking about the time REAL WORLD 4.3

5 Fill in the gaps with these words.

| ~~What~~ | It's | time | past | is | at | it | quarter |

A Excuse me. *What* time is _____ , please?
B _____ half _____ ten.

A What _____ _____ your English class?
B It's _____ to six.

Pronunciation: syllables and word stress (1)

6 Write these words in the table.

| ~~concert~~ computer |
| beautiful fifteen |
| fifty Saturday |
| tomato Chinese |
| umbrella address |
| office languages |

• • **foot**ball	• • six**teen**
concert	_____
_____	_____
_____	_____

• • • **news**paper	• • • ex**pen**sive
_____	_____
_____	_____
_____	_____

Spelling: double letters (1)

7 S Circle the words with the correct spelling.

1 smal / (small)
2 tisues / tissues
3 cinema / cinnema
4 shoping / shopping
5 magazine / maggazine
6 cofee / coffee
7 tenis / tennis
8 ugly / uggly
9 surname / surrname
10 bateries / batteries
11 manager / mannager
12 dolar / dollar

Reading and Writing Portfolio 4 p58

5A A typical day

Language Summary 5, Student's Book p122

Daily routines VOCABULARY 5.1

1 a S Mat Hunt is a doctor. Look at his daily routine. Write the phrases.

g et   u p

h_____
b_____

l_____ h_____

s_____ w_____

h_____ l_____

f_____ w_____

g_____ h_____

h_____ d_____

g_____ to b_____

s_____

b Write sentences about the times you do things in **1a**.

I get up at half past seven.

Present Simple (*he, she, it*): positive and negative GRAMMAR 5.1

2 Read about Mat Hunt's routine. Fill in the gaps with the correct positive (+) form of these verbs.

| ~~live~~ | finish | do | get up | sleep | read | leave |
| watch | start | get (x2) | go (x2) | have (x3) | | |

Mat Hunt is a doctor and he ¹ *lives* in Colchester, in the UK. In the week he ²_____ at 6.30. Mat and his wife, Sarah, ³_____ breakfast at about 7.00 with their two children, Josh and Ella. Mat ⁴_____ home at 7.15 and he ⁵_____ work at 7.30. He ⁶_____ lunch at about 1.15 and he ⁷_____ work at 6.30. He ⁸_____ home at about 6.45 and then he ⁹_____ dinner with his family. After dinner Josh and Ella ¹⁰_____ their homework and Mat ¹¹_____ TV or ¹²_____ the newspaper. He ¹³_____ to bed at 11.30 and he ¹⁴_____ for about seven hours. Mat and Sarah ¹⁵_____ out on Friday evening and they ¹⁶_____ home at about midnight.

3 Make these sentences negative. Write the correct sentences.

1 Mat lives in London.
   Mat doesn't live in London.
   He lives in Colchester.

2 He gets up at quarter to seven.
   _____
   _____

3 Mat and Sarah have three children.
   _____
   _____

4 Mat starts work at nine o'clock.
   _____
   _____

5 He finishes work at seven.
   _____
   _____

6 He goes to bed at half past ten.
   _____
   _____

7 Mat and Sarah go out on Thursday evening.
   _____
   _____

4 Choose the correct words.

1. Dylan *drink / drinks* a lot of coffee.
2. My brothers *love / loves* football.
3. Our parents *live / lives* in Mexico.
4. Jo and Dan *play / plays* tennis on Monday.
5. I *work / works* for a German car company.
6. My sister *like / likes* rock music.
7. My son *study / studies* Spanish at school.
8. We *eat / eats* out a lot at the weekend.
9. He *teach / teaches* English in Seoul.
10. They *play / plays* video games a lot.

Review: negatives (1)

5 Make these sentences negative.

1. I'm from the USA.
   I'm not from the USA.
2. I like vegetables.
3. They're my sister's friends.
4. He's a police officer.
5. Fiona works in an office.
6. My parents live in a flat.
7. We're from Australia.
8. My son has a new mobile.

5B Where does she work?

Time phrases with *on*, *in*, *at* VOCABULARY 5.2

1 Fill in the gaps with these words and phrases.

~~Wednesday~~   the morning   four o'clock   the afternoon   midday
Monday morning   half past five   Thursday afternoon   midnight
the evening   Sunday evening   night   the week   the weekend

on	in
Wednesday	

at

2 a Fill in the gaps with *on*, *in* or *at*.

1. I watch TV *in* the morning.
2. I sleep _____ the afternoon.
3. I have an English class _____ Monday evening.
4. I don't work _____ night.
5. I get up _____ seven o'clock _____ the week.
6. I have dinner _____ eight thirty _____ the evening.
7. I go to bed _____ midnight _____ the weekend.
8. I go shopping _____ Saturday morning.
9. I get up _____ midday _____ Sunday.
10. I watch TV _____ Sunday afternoon.

b Tick (✓) the sentences in **2a** that are true for you.

Present Simple (*he*, *she*, *it*): Wh- questions
GRAMMAR 5.2

3 a Look at the photo of Luke and the table. Fill in the gaps in questions 1–6.

Luke

Claire

	Luke	Claire
live	Brighton, UK	Miami, USA
work	English teacher in a language school	waitress in an Italian restaurant
get up	7.00 a.m.	11.00 a.m.
go to bed	11.30 p.m.	2.30 a.m.
free time	watch TV	play tennis
weekend	play football	go to concerts

1 Where _does_ Luke _live_?
  In Brighton, in the UK.
2 Where _____ he _____?
  In a language school.
3 What time _____ he _____ _____?
  At seven o'clock.
4 _____ time _____ he _____ to bed?
  At half past eleven.
5 What _____ he _____ in his free time?
  He watches TV.
6 _____ _____ he _____ at the weekend?
  He plays football.

b Look at the photo of Claire and the table in **3a**. Write the questions.

1 _Where does Claire live?_
  In Miami. In the USA.
2 _____ she _____
  In an Italian restaurant.
3 _____
  At eleven o'clock.
4 _____
  At half past two.
5 _____
  She plays tennis.
6 _____
  She goes to concerts.

Present Simple (*he*, *she*, *it*): yes / no questions and short answers
GRAMMAR 5.2

4 a Make questions with these words.

1 live / Luke / in the UK / Does ?
  Does Luke live in the UK?
2 Claire / Does / Brighton / in / live ?
  _____
3 get up / she / at / Does / eleven ?
  _____
4 at / to bed / Luke / ten thirty / go / Does ?
  _____
5 tennis / play / in / Does / Luke / his free time ?
  _____
6 Claire / Does / at / concerts / go to / the weekend ?
  _____

b Write short answers for the questions in **4a**.

1 _Yes, he does._   4 _____
2 _____   5 _____
3 _____   6 _____

Review: short answers

5 Write the positive (+) and negative (−) short answers.

1 Are you from Indonesia?
  (+) Yes, _I am._
  (−) No, _I'm not._
2 Do you like coffee?
  (+) Yes, _____
  (−) No, _____
3 Does your wife work at home?
  (+) _____
  (−) _____
4 Is her brother a doctor?
  (+) _____
  (−) _____
5 Are your sons married?
  (+) _____
  (−) _____
6 Do Tom and Mike live with their parents?
  (+) _____
  (−) _____

5C REAL WORLD — An evening out

Food and drink (3) VOCABULARY 5.3

1 ⓢ Do the crossword.

Polly   George

In a restaurant REAL WORLD 5.1

2 Look at the photo and read the conversation. Fill in the gaps with these phrases.

> ~~Are you ready~~   for me   a bottle of
> Can I have   Still, please   Not for me
> the bill   Of course   would you like

WAITRESS Good evening. ¹ *Are you ready* to order?
POLLY Yes. ² _____ the vegetable lasagne, please?
GEORGE And can I have the burger and chips?
WAITRESS Certainly. What ³ _____ to drink?
POLLY An orange juice for me, please.
GEORGE And can I have ⁴ _____ mineral water?
WAITRESS Still or sparkling?
GEORGE ⁵ _____ .
WAITRESS OK. Thanks very much.

WAITRESS Would you like a dessert?
POLLY ⁶ _____ , thanks.
GEORGE The fruit salad ⁷ _____ , please.
WAITRESS Certainly.

GEORGE Excuse me. Can we have ⁸ _____ , please?
WAITRESS ⁹ _____ .
GEORGE Thanks a lot.

5D VOCABULARY AND SKILLS — A day off

Frequency adverbs and phrases with every

VOCABULARY 5.4

1 a S Write the letters in these frequency adverbs.
1 n o t   us u a l l y
2 a _ w _ ys
3 n _ v _ r
4 s _ _ et _ _ es
5 u _ u _ _ ly

b Fill in the gaps with the frequency adverbs in **1a**.

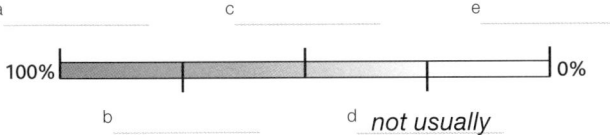

a _____ c _____ e _____
100% ────────────────── 0%
    b _____   d _not usually_

2 Put these phrases with *every* in order.

every year	every two hours
every minute 1	every ten years 8
every week	every six months
every month	every day

3 a Put the words in brackets ( ) in the correct place in these sentences.

    usually
1 I ⋏ go out on Monday evenings. (usually)
2 I eat out in the week. (don't usually)
3 I watch TV. (every evening)
4 I have breakfast in bed. (never)

5 I'm late for my English class. (sometimes)
6 I get up early. (every day)
7 I'm very busy in the week. (always)
8 I go to the cinema. (every weekend)

b Tick (✓) the sentences in **3a** that are true for you.

Pronunciation: sounds review (1)

HELP WITH PRONUNCIATION
Student's Book p13, p21, p29

4 Look at the letters in **bold** in these words. Write the words in the table.

m**a**n	**e**mail	teach**er**	m**u**ch	th**i**ng
d**o**ctor	**a**pple	sh**o**p	n**u**mber	**I**taly
h**o**t	s**i**ngle	pl**ea**se	pr**a**ctise	p**eo**ple
wom**a**n	l**o**ve	Br**i**tish		

/æ/	/ə/
bag	computer
man	

/ɪ/	/iː/
six	nineteen

/ɒ/	/ʌ/
coffee	umbrella

Spelling: Present Simple (*he*, *she*, *it*)

5 S Circle the correct spelling.
1 My father *gets* / *getes* home at eight.
2 Henrietta *finishs* / *finishes* work at 5.30.
3 Latif *studies* / *studys* languages.
4 Rob *works* / *workes* in an office.
5 Fred *watchs* / *watches* TV a lot.
6 He *gos* / *goes* to the cinema every weekend.
7 She *haves* / *has* three children.
8 The class *starts* / *startes* at ten o'clock.

Reading and Writing Portfolio 5 p60

6A My home town

Language Summary 6, Student's Book p124

Places in a town or city (1) VOCABULARY 6.1

1 a Write the vowels (*a, e, i, o, u*) in these words for places in a town or city.

a a b _u_ _i_ ld _i_ ng
b a sh __ pp __ ng c __ ntr __
c a m __ s __ m
d a r __ v __ r
e a b __ s st __ t __ __ n
f a p __ rk
g a th __ __ tr __
h an __ __ rp __ rt
i a st __ t __ __ n

b Look at the map of Rushley, a town in the UK. Match the words in **1a** to places 1–9 on the map.

a _1_   d ___   g ___
b ___   e ___   h ___
c ___   f ___   i ___

a, some, a lot of; *there is / there are*: positive
GRAMMAR 6.1

2 Read these sentences about Rushley. Fill in the gaps with *There's* or *There are*.

1 _There's_ a café near the bus station.
2 _____ two very nice parks.
3 _____ a cinema in Rushley.
4 _____ two four-star hotels.
5 _____ a big shopping centre.
6 _____ a lot of good shops.
7 _____ some beautiful buildings.
8 _____ an Italian restaurant called Silvio's.
9 _____ an airport near Rushley.
10 _____ a café in the airport.
11 _____ some famous pictures in the museum.
12 _____ a very good theatre.
13 _____ a lot of friendly people in Rushley.
14 _____ some nice houses near the town.

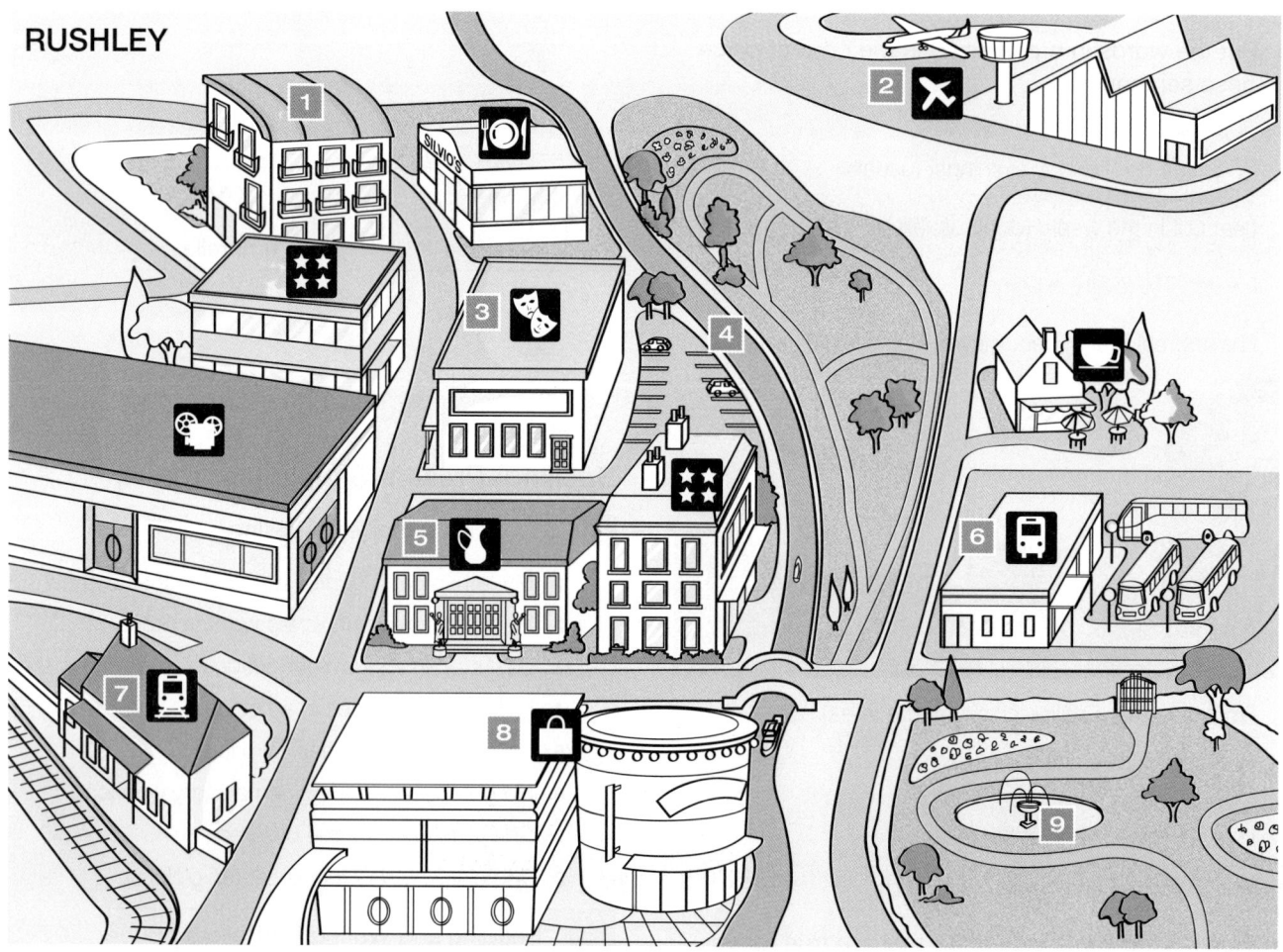

28

3 Choose the correct words. Then tick (✓) the sentences that are true for you.

Near my house or flat
1 There's (a) / some station.
2 There's a / a lot of park.
3 There are a / a lot of shops.
4 There's a / an old theatre.
5 There are a / two cinemas.
6 There are a / some good restaurants.

In my town or city
7 There's a / some river.
8 There are some / a famous buildings.
9 There's a lot of / an airport.
10 There are an / a lot of nice cafés.
11 There's a / a lot of big shopping centre.
12 There are a / some expensive hotels.

Review: there, they're, their

4 a Read these sentences. Notice the difference between *there*, *they're* and *their*.

1 **There** are some good museums.
2 **They're** from France. (*they're = they are*)
3 This is **their** house. (*their* + noun)

TIP • We use the same pronunciation for *there*, *they're* and *their* /ðeə/.

b [S] Fill in the gaps with *there*, *they're* or *their*.

1 _There_ 's a great restaurant near my flat.
2 _____ from Tripoli, in Libya.
3 What are _____ names?
4 _____ are about 50 people in the company.
5 Can you tell me _____ phone number?
6 I like these pictures. _____ very beautiful.
7 _____ are twelve people in our class.

6B Are there any shops?

Places in a town or city (2) VOCABULARY 6.2

1 [S] Write the letters in these words for places in a town or city.

a c h e m i s t ' s

a m _ _ _ _ _ _ _

a p _ _ _ o _ _ _ _ _ _

a r _ _ _ _

a b _ _ s _ _ _ _

a b _ _ _ _

a s _ _ _ _ _ _

a c _ _ _ _ _ _ _ _

a s _ _ _ _ _ _ _

there is / there are: positive and negative GRAMMAR 6.1 GRAMMAR 6.2

2 Read about where Henry lives. Fill in the gaps with *there's*, *there isn't*, *there are* or *there aren't*.

Henry

I live in Greenwich, in London. ¹ _There are_ (+) a lot of things to do here. ² _____ (+) a lot of nice old buildings, some very good museums and ³ _____ (+) a very beautiful park.

⁴ _____ (−) a big shopping centre in the centre of Greenwich, but ⁵ _____ (+) a lot of nice shops. ⁶ _____ (+) also two theatres and a cinema. ⁷ _____ (+) a famous market in Greenwich 5 days a week, but ⁸ _____ (−) a market on Monday or Tuesday.

I live about ten minutes from Greenwich station. ⁹ _____ (+) a supermarket near the station, but ¹⁰ _____ (−) any shops in my road. And ¹¹ _____ (−) any restaurants near my flat, but ¹² _____ (+) a lot of very good restaurants in the centre. I think Greenwich is a great place to live.

there is / there are: yes / no questions and short answers
GRAMMAR 6.2

3 Make questions about Greenwich with these words.

1 a / Is / park / there ?
   Is there a park?

2 good / any / museums / Are / there ?
   _____

3 big / there / shopping centre / Is / a ?
   _____

4 Tuesdays / there / on / market / Is / a ?
   _____

5 Are / Henry's road / in / there / shops / any ?
   _____

6 a / there / the station / near / Is / supermarket ?
   _____

7 Henry's flat / any / there / near / restaurants / Are ?
   _____

8 in / restaurants / good / any / Are / the centre / there ?
   _____

4 Read about Greenwich again. Then write the short answers to the questions in **3**.

1 _Yes, there is._
2 _____
3 _____
4 _____
5 _____
6 _____
7 _____
8 _____

a, some, a lot of; any GRAMMAR 6.1
GRAMMAR 6.2

5 Choose the correct words.

1 There's ⓐ / *some* post office.
2 Are there *a* / *any* shops?
3 There isn't *a* / *any* theatre.
4 There are *any* / *some* nice cafés.
5 There aren't *any* / *an* old buildings.
6 There's *an* / *any* airport.
7 Are there *an* / *any* museums?
8 There are *some* / *any* restaurants.

6C REAL WORLD Tourist information

Things in your bag (2) VOCABULARY 6.3

1 S Do the crossword.

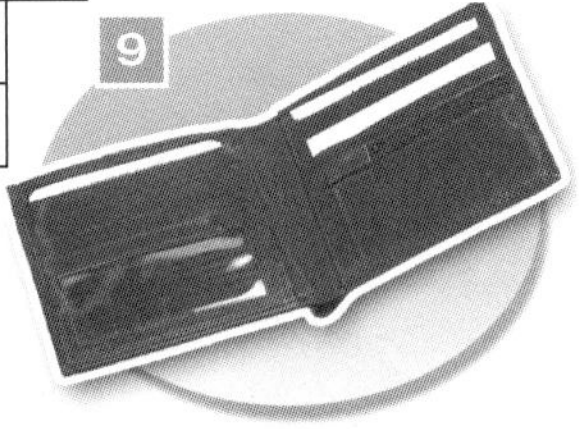

Across: 1 ID CARD ...

At the tourist information centre
REAL WORLD 6.1

2 Romina (R) is at the tourist information centre in Greenwich. Put her conversation with the assistant (A) in order.

- a R Thank you. And can I book a walking tour here?
- b R OK. How much are they?
- c R Yes, please. Do you have a map of Greenwich? **2**
- d A They're £7.00 per person.
- e A Hello, can I help you? **1**
- f A Yes, you can. They're at 12.15 and 2.15.
- g A Yes, of course. Here you are.
- h R Is it open every day?
- i R OK, thanks. Also, where's the Greenwich Theatre?
- j R And when is the Maritime Museum open? **8**
- k R Thanks a lot. Goodbye.
- l R Can you show me on this map?
- m A Yes, it is.
- n A It's open from 10 a.m. to 5 p.m.
- o A Yes, of course. Here it is. It's about five minutes away.
- p A It's in Crooms Hill.

3 Read the conversation in **2** again. Answer these questions.

1 Does the tourist information centre have maps of Greenwich?
   Yes, it does.
2 How much are the walking tours of Greenwich?
   _____
3 What time is the Maritime Museum open?
   _____
4 Is it open on Sundays?
   _____
5 Where is the Greenwich Theatre?
   _____
6 Is the Greenwich Theatre near the tourist information centre?
   _____

VOCABULARY 6D AND SKILLS It's my favourite

Clothes
VOCABULARY 6.4

1 [S] Write the words.

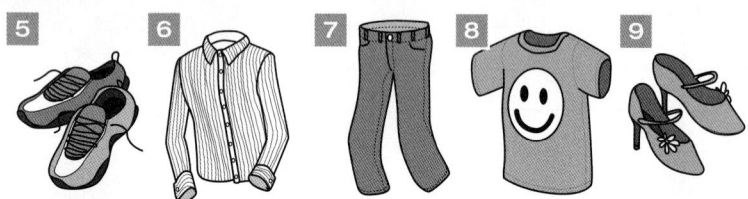

1 a t _i_ _e_
2 b _ _ _ s
3 a j _ _ _ _ r
4 a c _ _ t
5 t _ _ _ _ s
6 a s _ _ _ _ t
7 j _ _ _ _ s
8 a T- _ _ _ _ t
9 s _ _ _ s
10 t _ _ _ _ _ _ s
11 a s _ _ _ _ t
12 a j _ _ _ _ t
13 a d _ _ _ s
14 a s _ _ t

Colours VOCABULARY 6.5

2 [S] Write the colours.

1 der   r _ed_
2 loeywl   y _____
3 ronwb   b _____
4 cabkl   b _____
5 enrge   g _____
6 elub   b _____
7 tihew   w _____
8 ipkn   p _____
9 eyrg   g _____

favourite VOCABULARY 6.6

3 Make sentences with these words.

1 favourite / your / food / What's ?
   What's your favourite food?

2 are / shoes / These / favourite / my .
   _____

3 singer / your / favourite / Who's ?
   _____

4 favourite / my / is / This / shirt .
   _____

5 blue / favourite / My / is / colour .
   _____

Pronunciation: /tʃ/ and /dʒ/

HELP WITH PRONUNCIATION Student's Book p53

4 a Look at these pictures. Check you remember the sounds /tʃ/ and /dʒ/.

cheese /tʃ/

orange juice /dʒ/

b Look at the letters in **bold**. Circle the correct sounds.

1 **ch**ocolate   (/tʃ/)   /dʒ/
2 **j**umper   /tʃ/   (/dʒ/)
3 langua**ge**   /tʃ/   /dʒ/
4 **ch**ildren   /tʃ/   /dʒ/
5 mana**g**er   /tʃ/   /dʒ/
6 pic**t**ure   /tʃ/   /dʒ/
7 **j**eans   /tʃ/   /dʒ/
8 Fren**ch**   /tʃ/   /dʒ/
9 pa**ge**   /tʃ/   /dʒ/
10 mu**ch**   /tʃ/   /dʒ/
11 **ch**ips   /tʃ/   /dʒ/
12 **j**acket   /tʃ/   /dʒ/

Spelling: silent letters (1)

5 [S] We don't say every letter in some words. Write the silent letters.

1   su _i_ t
2   lis _t_ en
3   b __ ilding
4   theat __ e
5   __ rite
6   ans __ er
7   san __ wich
8   We __ nesday
9   pos __ card
10 bre __ kfast
11 veg __ tables
12 fru __ t
13 bre __ d
14 choc __ late

Reading and Writing Portfolio 6 p62

7A We're twins

Language Summary 7, Student's Book p126

Things you like and don't like
VOCABULARY 7.1

1 Write the letters in these words.

1 s o a p   o p e r a s
2 a _ _ m _ _ s
3 v _ _ _ t _ _ g new pl _ _ _ s
4 d _ _ c _ _ g
5 h _ rr _ _ f _ _ _ s
6 s _ _ pp _ _ g for c _ _ th _ _
7 f _ y _ _ g
8 cl _ ss _ _ _ l m _ _ _ c
9 w _ _ ch _ ng sp _ _ t on T _

love, like, don't like, hate
VOCABULARY 7.2

2 Match these phrases to the pictures.

| I love | I hate | I don't like | I like |

1 _____   3 _____
2 _____   4 _____

3 Mel and Andy are twins. Look at the photos and the table. Then fill in the gaps in sentences 1–12.

1 Mel _loves_ cats.
2 She _____ classical music.
3 She _____ _____ football.
4 She _____ watching sport on TV.
5 Andy _____ dancing.
6 He _____ rock _____ .
7 He _____ like tennis.
8 He _____ horror _____ .
9 Andy and Mel _____ ice _____ .
10 They _____ Chinese _____ .
11 They _____ coffee.
12 They _____ flying.

33

Object pronouns GRAMMAR 7.1

4 Change the words in **bold** to object pronouns.

1 I like classical music, but Ian hates ~~classical music~~. *it*
2 A Do you know Kim's brother?
   B Yes, but I don't like **Kim's brother**. _____
3 I don't like dogs, but my husband loves **dogs**. _____
4 A Does Adela love Chris?
   B Yes, and Chris loves **Adela**! _____
5 I don't like flying, but my wife loves **flying**. _____
6 Ed and I like Jo, but she doesn't like **Ed and me**. _____

Review: subject and object pronouns

5 Choose the correct words.

1 Is (he) / him in this class?
2 I / me phone he / him every day.
3 We / Us don't know they / them.
4 Do they / them know she / her?
5 She / Her plays tennis with I / me.
6 He / Him never talks to we / us.

Review: Present Simple

6 Correct the mistakes.

            do you
1 Where ~~you do~~ live?
2 Fiona don't work in an office.
3 Where do your daughter live?
4 Lin study English at a language school in London.
5 What does your parents do in the evening?
6 Lydia and Pia doesn't like soap operas.
7 My brother haves three cars.
8 Tom's son work for a computer company.
9 Jack watchs TV every evening.
10 What time do you starts work?

7B Can you drive?

Abilities VOCABULARY 7.3

1 Do the crossword.

play the _____

_____ a bike

play the _____

_____ Italian

_____ basketball

can: positive and negative GRAMMAR 7.2

2 Fill in the gaps with *can* or *can't* and these verbs.

> ~~play~~   ski   cook   sing   speak

1 Mark _can't_ _play_ football.

2 They _____ .

3 Tamara _____ .

4 She _____ very well.

5 They _____ Russian.

can: yes / no questions and short answers GRAMMAR 7.3

3 Make questions with these words. Then write the positive (+) and negative (−) short answers.

1 understand / Spanish / you / Can ?
   Can you understand Spanish?
   (+) _Yes, I can._
   (−) _No, I can't._

2 drive / your / sister / Can ?
   _____
   (+) _____
   (−) _____

3 French / your / Can / speak / parents ?
   _____
   (+) _____
   (−) _____

4 the piano / son / play / your / Can ?
   _____
   (+) _____
   (−) _____

5 this / you / exercise / Can / do ?
   _____
   (+) _____
   (−) _____

Review: vocabulary

4 **S** Find fifteen words (→↓). Write the words in the table. There are five words for each group.

T	H	E	A	T	R	E	M	Q	P
R	M	A	W	B	A	X	U	L	A
E	A	W	H	K	E	Y	S	B	S
D	P	E	I	P	M	Z	E	L	S
S	T	A	T	I	O	N	U	A	P
O	J	U	E	N	N	A	M	C	O
P	A	R	K	K	E	H	E	K	R
M	O	G	R	E	Y	N	O	B	T
L	J	Y	S	Q	U	A	R	E	C
C	R	E	D	I	T	C	A	R	D

places in a town or city	things in your bag	colours
theatre		

7C REAL WORLD > Directions

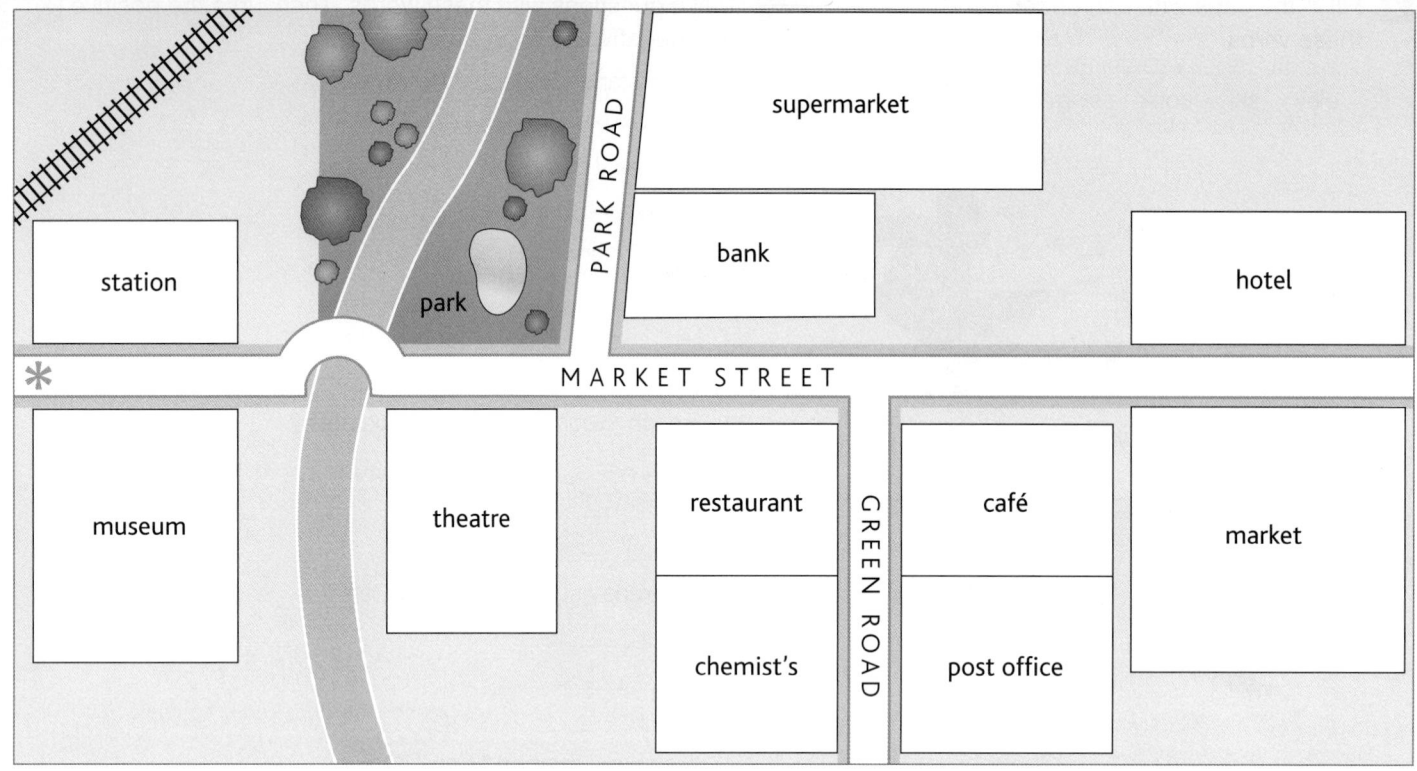

Prepositions of place VOCABULARY 7.4

1 You are at ✳ on the map. Choose the correct words.

1 The station is *on* / *in* the left.
2 The café is *next to* / *opposite* the restaurant.
3 The post office is *next to* / *opposite* the café.
4 The hotel is *in* / *near* Market Street.
5 The museum is *in* / *on* your right.
6 The bank is *near* / *in* the theatre.
7 The market is *next to* / *opposite* the hotel.
8 The restaurant is *next to* / *opposite* the chemist's.

Asking for and giving directions REAL WORLD 7.1

2 You are at ✳ on the map. Read these directions. Write the places.

1 It's over there, opposite the theatre. *the park*
2 Go along this road and turn right. It's on your right, next to the restaurant. _____
3 Go along this road and turn left. It's on your right, next to the supermarket. _____
4 Go along this road. It's on your left, opposite the market. _____
5 Go along this road and turn right. It's on your right, opposite the café. _____

3 Penny is at ✳ on the map. Fill in the gaps with these words and phrases.

| ~~Excuse me~~   on the left   That's |
| opposite   Go along |

PENNY ¹ *Excuse me* . Where's the post office?
MAN ² _____ this road and turn right. ³ _____ Green Road. The post office is ⁴ _____ , ⁵ _____ the chemist's.
PENNY Thank you very much.
MAN You're welcome.

| next to   on your right   near here |
| turn left   Is there |

PENNY Excuse me. ⁶ _____ a supermarket ⁷ _____ ?
WOMAN Yes, there is. Go along this road and ⁸ _____ . The supermarket is ⁹ _____ , ¹⁰ _____ the bank.
PENNY Thanks a lot.
WOMAN No problem.

Answer Key

1A What's your name?

1 PAULA   Hello, I'm Paula. **What's your** name?
   ENZO   Hello, **my name's** Enzo.
   PAULA   Nice **to meet** you.
   ENZO   **You too.**
   LENA   Hi, Amir.
   AMIR   Hi, Lena. **How are** you?
   LENA   **I'm fine,** thanks. **And you?**
   AMIR   I'm OK, **thanks.**
2 YVONNE Robert, **this** is Meilin.
   ROBERT **Hello,** Meilin. **Nice to meet** you.
   MEILIN You **too.**
3 LENA   **Bye,** Amir.
   AMIR   **Goodbye,** Lena. **See** you **soon.**
   LENA   **Yes, see** you.
4 HUGO   Hello, I'm Hugo. **What's your** name?
   LIAN   Hi, **my** name's Lian.
   HUGO   Nice to meet **you.**
   LIAN   **You too.**
   CARLA   Hello, Alexei.
   ALEXEI Hi, Carla. How are **you?**
   CARLA   I'm fine, thanks. And **you?**
   ALEXEI I'm OK, thanks.
5 1 one   2 two   3 three   4 four
   5 five 6 six   7 seven   8 eight
   9 nine 10 ten 11 eleven
   12 twelve
6 **What's your mobile** number?
   It's 07700 900187.
   What's **your** home **number?**
   It's 0121 496 0317.

1B Where's she from?

1 2 Italy 3 Australia 4 the USA
   5 Brazil 6 Spain 7 China
   8 Germany 9 Turkey 10 the UK
   11 Mexico 12 Russia
2 FABIEN Hello, I'm Fabien.
   CLARA   Hi, **my name's** Clara.
   FABIEN **Nice** to **meet** you.
   CLARA   You **too.**
   FABIEN **Where** are you from?
   CLARA   **I'm from** Spain. **And** you?
   FABIEN **I'm** from France.
3 EMMA   Hi, Brian.
   BRIAN   Hello, Emma. **How** are you?
   EMMA   I'm fine, **thanks.** And **you?**
   BRIAN   I'm **OK,** thanks.
   EMMA   Brian, **this** is Kaoru.
   BRIAN   Hello, Kaoru. **Nice** to meet you.
   KAORU   You **too.**
   EMMA   Where are you **from?**
   KAORU   I'm from Osaka, in Japan.
4 2 He 3 Her 4 She 5 his 6 His
   7 he 8 He 9 her 10 Her 11 she
   12 She

1C In class

1a a b c d **e** f g h i j k l m
    n o p q r s t u v w x y z
 b D E F G H I J K L M N O P
    Q R S T U V W X Y Z
2 TEACHER What's **your** first **name,** please?
   ANTONIO It's Antonio.
   TEACHER **What's** your **surname?**
   ANTONIO Morales.
   TEACHER **How** do you **spell** that?
   ANTONIO M–o–r–a–l–e–s.
3 2 a pencil 3 a mobile
   4 a notebook 5 an umbrella
   6 a bag 7 a pen 8 a book
   9 an apple
4 2 How do you spell 3 What does
   4 I don't understand 5 Can you repeat that 6 in English 7 I don't know

1D People and things

1 2 table 3 sandwich 4 woman
   5 baby 6→ camera 6↓ computer
   7 boy 8 man 9 diary 10 chair
   11 girl
2 2 teachers 3 people 4 things
   5 babies 6 men 7 names
   8 countries 9 sandwiches
   10 women 11 watches 12 answers
3 2 Brazil 3 Russia 4 Germany
   5 Australia 6 Turkey 7 computer
   8 notebook 9 dictionary
   10 umbrella 11 apple 12 mobile
4 /æ/ apple, practise, vocabulary, sandwich
   /ə/ China, woman, Brazil, Italy
5 2 eight 3 pencil 4 umbrella
   5 phone 6 notebook 7 sorry
   8 sandwich 9 surname
   10 first name

2A She's British

1 [word search grid]

2 2 's 3 's 4 's 5 'm 6 'm 7 're
   8 's 9 'm 10 'm 11 's
3 2 He isn't a student. / He's not a student. 3 You aren't from Russia. / You're not from Russia. 4 It isn't German. / It's not German. 5 She isn't Chinese. / She's not Chinese. 6 I'm not British. 7 My teacher isn't American. / My teacher's not American. 8 You aren't a singer. / You're not a singer.
4 3 Cameron Diaz isn't from Spain. She's from the USA. 4 ✓ 5 Big Ben isn't in Washington. It's in London. 6 Daniel Craig isn't Russian. He's British. 7 Starbucks isn't a British company. It's an American company. 8 ✓

2B What's your job?

1 2 an actress 3 an actor
   4 a taxi driver 5 a sales assistant
   6 a musician 7 a police officer
   8 a waitress 9 a waiter
   10 a doctor 11 a teacher
2 Conversation 1
   A Hello, **what's** your name?
   B **My name's** Oliver.
   A Where **are** you from?
   B I'm from the UK.
   A **What's** your job?
   B I'm an actor.
   Conversation 2
   A Hi, **what's** your name?
   B My **name's** Holly.
   A Where are you **from?**
   B I'm from the USA.
   A What's your **job?**
   B I'm an actress.
3 1 A What's his name?
     B His **name's** Bruce.
     A Where's he from?
     B He's from Australia.
     A What's his job?
     B He's a waiter.
   2 A What's her name?
     B Her name's Aylin.
     A Where's she from?
     B She's from Turkey.
     A What's her job?
     B She's a doctor.
   3 A What's his name?
     B His name's Hamadi.
     A Where's he from?
     B He's from Egypt.
     A What's his job?
     B He's a manager.
   4 A What's her name?
     B Her name's Carolina.
     A Where's she from?

Answer Key

   B She's from Mexico.
   A What's her job?
   B She's a teacher.

4a 2 Is he a police officer? 3 Is Aylin from Germany? 4 Is she a doctor? 5 Is Hamadi from France? 6 Is he a manager? 7 Is Carolina from Mexico? 8 Is she a waitress?

b 2 No, he isn't. / No, he's not. 3 No, she isn't. / No, she's not. 4 Yes, she is. 5 No, he isn't. / No, he's not. 6 Yes, he is. 7 Yes, she is. 8 No, she isn't. / No, she's not.

5 1 A **Am** I in this class?
    B Yes, you **are**.
  2 A **Are** you Russian?
    B Yes, I **am**.
  3 A **Is** your car Japanese?
    B No, it **isn't**.
  4 A **Are** you a musician?
    B No, **I'm** not.
  5 A **Is** this your bag?
    B Yes, it **is**.

2C Personal information

1 1 Good morning 2 Good morning 3 Good night 4 Good night 5 Good afternoon 6 Mrs 7 Good afternoon 8 Good evening 9 Mr 10 Good evening

2 2 What's your surname? 3 How do you spell that? 4 What's your nationality? 5 What's your address? 6 Can you repeat that, please? 7 What's your email address? 8 What's your mobile number?

2D How old is she?

1 b thirty c fourteen d forty e fifteen f fifty g sixteen h sixty i seventeen j seventy k eighteen l eighty m nineteen n ninety

2 b seventy-seven c twenty-six d forty-two e fifty-one f a hundred

3 1 How old 2 years 3 How old are 4 I'm 5 How old is 6 He's

4 2 Russian 3 American 4 British 5 Chinese 6 Spanish 7 Brazilian 8 Italian 9 Turkish 10 Australian

5b 3 D 4 S 5 D 6 D 7 S 8 S 9 D 10 D

6 2 a waiter 3 a waitress 4 a doctor 5 an actor 6 an actress 7 a taxi driver 8 a manager

7 2 diaries 3 girls 4 watches 5 countries 6 sandwiches 7 babies 8 men 9 women 10 people

3A Two cities

1a 2 hot 3 new 4 small 5 friendly 6 beautiful 7 expensive

b 2 cold 3 old 4 big 5 unfriendly 6 ugly 7 cheap

2 2 My teacher is very friendly. 3 It's a very old phone. 4 She's a good doctor. 5 The bags are expensive. 6 It's a very big house. 7 Egypt is a hot country. 8 The sandwiches are very nice. 9 His dictionary is very good.

3 2 're 3 's 4 are 5 aren't / 're not 6 're 7 isn't / 's not 8 's (is) 9 aren't / 're not 10 're 11 isn't / 's not 12 's 13 's

4a 2 Are 3 Are 4 's (is) 5 Is 6 Are 7 's (is) 8 Is

b 2 Yes, they are. 3 No, they aren't. / No, they're not. 4 It's in Chiang Mai. 5 No, it isn't. / No, it's not. 6 No, they aren't. / No, they're not. 7 He's in a café. 8 Yes, it is.

5 2 I'm from Moscow. 3 You aren't in this class. / You're not in this class. 4 He isn't from London. / He's not from London. 5 What's your name? 6 She isn't Spanish, she's Mexican. / She's not Spanish, she's Mexican. 7 We're in Poland and it's very cold. 8 They aren't actors, they're waiters. / They're not actors, they're waiters.

6 2 c 3 b 4 c 5 a 6 b 7 c 8 a

3B Brothers and sisters

1 2 son 3 husband 4 daughter 5 wife 6 sister 7 mother 8 brother 9 parents 10 children

2 2 granddaughter 3 grandmother 4 grandson 5 grandfather 6 grandchildren

3 2 Frank's 3 Rita's 4 Joe's 5 Frank's 6 Rita's 7 Daisy's 8 Jane's

4 3 is 4 is 5 P 6 P 7 is 8 P

5 **subject pronouns: I, you, he, she, it, we, they**
possessive adjectives: my, your, his, her, its, our, their

6 2 our 3 his 4 We 5 your 6 My, her 7 It 8 their 9 They, his 10 she, your

7 2 are 3 's (is) 4 's (is) 5 Are 6 aren't / 're not 7 's (is) 8 's (is) 9 Are 10 'm 11 are 12 'm 13 're 14 Is 15 isn't / 's not 16 's

3C Eat in or take away?

1 2 a mineral water 3 an egg sandwich 4 a tuna salad 5 a tea 6 a coffee 7 an orange juice 8 a croissant 9 a cappuccino 10 a cheese and tomato sandwich

2 b seven euros c twenty cents d fifteen pounds e twenty-five p / pence f nine (pounds) seventy

3 1 How much is 2 How much are 3 How much are 4 How much is

4 ASSISTANT **Can** I **help** you?
CUSTOMER 1 Yes, a coffee and a croissant, **please**.
A Sure. **Anything** else?
C1 No, that's all, thanks.
A Eat **in** or **take** **away**?
C1 **Eat** in, please.
A OK, **that's** £3.50, please.
C1 **Thanks** a lot.
A You're **welcome**.

ASSISTANT **Can** I **help** you?
CUSTOMER 2 Yes, a cappuccino, please.
A **Sure**. Anything **else**?
C2 Yes, an egg sandwich, **please**.
A **Eat** in or **take** away?
C2 Take **away**, please.
A OK, that's £4.75, please.
C2 **Thank** you very **much**.
A You're welcome.

3D Food I like

1 2 chocolate 3 cheese 4 fish 5 vegetables 6 orange juice 7 sugar 8 bread 9 eggs 10 meat 11 pasta 12 water 13 tea 14 coffee 15 fruit 16 milk

2a 1 like 2 drink, lot 3 eat, lot 4 love

3b b 3 c 1 d 3 e 2 f 3 g 2 h 1 i 2 j 3

4b 3 /ʌ/ 4 /ɒ/ 5 /ɒ/ 6 /ʌ/ 7 /ɒ/ 8 /ɒ/ 9 /ʌ/ 10 /ʌ/

5 b fifteen c fifty-six d fourteen e forty f twenty-eight g ninety-nine h eleven i twelve j eighty-three k thirty-one l a hundred

4A Live, work and study

1 2 **work** in an **office** 3 like **football** 4 **live** in a **flat** 5 study **languages** 6 **like** rock **music** 7 have a **car** 8 live in the **centre** of the **city** 9 **have** two **children** 10 work for a **British company**

2 2 have 3 don't have 4 study 5 like 6 don't like 7 live 8 work 9 don't have 10 have

Answer Key

3a 2 like 3 have 4 live 5 study
  6 live 7 have 8 work 9 like
b Students' answers

4B My free time

1a 2 play tennis 3 go out with friends
  4 play video games 5 go to the cinema 6 eat out 7 go to concerts
  8 go shopping
2 1 live 2 have 4 watch 5 play
  6 eat 7 love 8 eat 9 drink
3 2 Do they like Chicago?
  3 What music do they like?
  4 What do they do in their free time?
  5 Do they eat out a lot?
  6 What food do they like?
  7 Do they eat a lot of sandwiches?
  8 Do they drink a lot of coffee?
4 2 Do I know you? No, you don't.
  3 Do you work in an office? Yes, I do. (Yes, we do.) 4 Do you have a big flat? No, I don't. (No, we don't.)
  5 Do we have a class today? Yes, we do. / Yes, you do. 6 Do Pete and Andy like football? Yes, they do.
  7 Do your parents have a car? No, they don't.

4C Buying things

1 2 magazine 3 sweets 4 tissues
  5 map 6 chocolates 7 postcard
  8 batteries 9 birthday card
  thing to buy (↓): newspaper
2 2 That 3 those 4 these 5 this
  6 that
3a 2 Do you have 3 How much are
  4 can I have 5 No, that's all
  6 Here you are 7 Goodbye
b £4.50

4D What time is it?

1 2 Tuesday 3 Wednesday
  4 Thursday 5 Friday
  6 Saturday 7 Sunday
2 a minutes b hour c days
  d weeks e year f months
3 2 quarter past five, five fifteen
  3 half past ten, ten thirty
  4 quarter to three, two forty-five
4 2 five to six 3 twenty to four
  4 twenty-five past two 5 ten to seven 6 five past eleven
  7 twenty-five to twelve
  8 twenty past one
5 1 A What time is it, please?
      B It's half past ten.
  2 A What time is your English class?
      B It's at quarter to six.

6

●●	●●
football	six**teen**
concert	fifteen
fifty	Chinese
office	address

●●●	●●●
newspaper	ex**pen**sive
beautiful	computer
Saturday	tomato
languages	umbrella

7 2 tissues 3 cinema 4 shopping
  5 magazine 6 coffee 7 tennis
  8 ugly 9 surname 10 batteries
  11 manager 12 dollar

5A A typical day

1a 2 have breakfast 3 leave home
  4 start work 5 have lunch
  6 finish work 7 get home
  8 have dinner 9 go to bed 10 sleep
b Students' answers
2 2 gets up 3 have 4 leaves
  5 starts 6 has 7 finishes 8 gets
  9 has 10 do 11 watches 12 reads
  13 goes 14 sleeps 15 go 16 get
3 2 He doesn't get up at quarter to seven. He gets up at half past six / six thirty / 6.30.
  3 Mat and Sarah don't have three children. They have two children.
  4 Mat doesn't start work at nine o'clock. He starts work at half past seven / seven thirty / 7.30.
  5 He doesn't finish work at seven. He finishes work at half past six / six thirty / 6.30.
  6 He doesn't go to bed at half past ten. He goes to bed at half past eleven / eleven thirty / 11.30.
  7 Mat and Sarah don't go out on Thursday evening. They go out on Friday evening.
4 2 love 3 live 4 play 5 work
  6 likes 7 studies 8 eat 9 teaches
  10 play
5 2 I don't like vegetables. 3 They aren't my sister's friends. / They're not my sister's friends. 4 He isn't a police officer. / He's not a police officer. 5 Fiona doesn't work in an office. 6 My parents don't live in a flat. 7 We aren't from Australia. / We're not from Australia. 8 My son doesn't have a new mobile.

5B Where does she work?

1

on	Monday morning Thursday afternoon Sunday evening
in	the morning the afternoon the evening the week
at	four o'clock midday half past five midnight night the weekend

2a 2 in 3 on 4 at 5 at, in 6 at, in
  7 at, at 8 on 9 at, on 10 on
3a 2 Where does he work?
  3 What time does he get up?
  4 What time does he go to bed?
  5 What does he do in his free time?
  6 What does he do at the weekend?
b 2 Where does she work?
  3 What time does she get up?
  4 What time does she go to bed?
  5 What does she do in her free time?
  6 What does she do at the weekend?
4a 2 Does Claire live in Brighton?
  3 Does she get up at eleven?
  4 Does Luke go to bed at ten thirty?
  5 Does Luke play tennis in his free time?
  6 Does Claire go to concerts at the weekend?
b 2 No, she doesn't. 3 Yes, she does.
  4 No, he doesn't. 5 No, he doesn't.
  6 Yes, she does.
5 2 Yes, I do. No, I don't. 3 Yes, she does. No, she doesn't. 4 Yes, he is. No, he isn't. / No, he's not. 5 Yes, they are. No, they aren't. / No, they're not. 6 Yes, they do. No, they don't.

5C An evening out

1 1→ mushroom 1↓ mineral water
  2 cream 3 coffee 4 burger
  5 lasagne 6 fruit salad 7 vanilla ice cream 8 apple pie 9 salad
  10 chips 11 strawberry 12 chicken
  13 pizza
2 2 Can I have 3 would you like
  4 a bottle of 5 Still, please
  6 Not for me 7 for me 8 the bill
  9 Of course

Answer Key

5D A day off

1a 2 always 3 never 4 sometimes 5 usually

b a always b usually c sometimes e never

2 1 every minute 2 every two hours 3 every day 4 every week 5 every month 6 every six months 7 every year 8 every ten years

3a 2 I **don't usually** eat out in the week.
3 I watch TV **every evening**.
4 I **never** have breakfast in bed.
5 I'm **sometimes** late for my English class.
6 I get up early **every day**.
7 I'm **always** very busy in the week.
8 I go to the cinema **every weekend**.

4

/æ/	/ə/
bag	computer
man	teacher
apple	Italy
practise	woman

/ɪ/	/iː/
six	nineteen
thing	email
single	please
British	people

/ɒ/	/ʌ/
coffee	umbrella
doctor	much
shop	number
hot	love

5 2 finishes 3 studies 4 works 5 watches 6 goes 7 has 8 starts

6A My home town

1a b a shopping centre c a museum d a river e a bus station f a park g a theatre h an airport i a station

b b 8 c 5 d 4 e 6 f 9 g 3 h 2 i 7

2 2 There are 3 There's 4 There are 5 There's 6 There are 7 There are 8 There's 9 There's 10 There's 11 There are 12 There's 13 There are 14 There are

3 2 a 3 a lot of 4 an 5 two 6 some 7 a 8 some 9 an 10 a lot of 11 a 12 some

4b 2 They're 3 their 4 There 5 their 6 They're 7 There

6B Are there any shops?

1 2 a market 3 a post office 4 a road 5 a bus stop 6 a bank 7 a square 8 a cashpoint 9 a supermarket

2 2 There are 3 there's 4 There isn't 5 there are 6 There are 7 There's 8 there isn't 9 There's 10 there aren't 11 there aren't 12 there are

3 2 Are there any good museums?
3 Is there a big shopping centre?
4 Is there a market on Tuesdays?
5 Are there any shops in Henry's road?
6 Is there a supermarket near the station?
7 Are there any restaurants near Henry's flat?
8 Are there any good restaurants in the centre?

4 2 Yes, there are. 3 No, there isn't. 4 No, there isn't. 5 No, there aren't. 6 Yes, there is. 7 No, there aren't. 8 Yes, there are.

5 2 any 3 a 4 some 5 any 6 an 7 any 8 some

6C Tourist information

1 2 credit card 3 purse 4 guide book 5 camera 6 money 7 keys 8 laptop 9 wallet 10 passport 11 map

2 1 e 2 c 3 g 4 a 5 f 6 b 7 d 8 j 9 n 10 h 11 m 12 i 13 p 14 l 15 o 16 k

3 2 They're £7.00 / seven pounds per person. 3 From 10 a.m. to 5 p.m. 4 Yes, it is. 5 (It's in) Crooms Hill. 6 Yes, it is.

6D It's my favourite

1 2 boots 3 a jumper 4 a coat 5 trainers 6 a shirt 7 jeans 8 a T-shirt 9 shoes 10 trousers 11 a skirt 12 a jacket 13 a dress 14 a suit

2 2 yellow 3 brown 4 black 5 green 6 blue 7 white 8 pink 9 grey

3 2 These are my favourite shoes.
3 Who's your favourite singer?
4 This is my favourite shirt.
5 My favourite colour is blue.

4b 3 /dʒ/ 4 /tʃ/ 5 /dʒ/ 6 /tʃ/ 7 /dʒ/ 8 /tʃ/ 9 /dʒ/ 10 /tʃ/ 11 /tʃ/ 12 /dʒ/

5 3 building 4 theatre 5 write 6 answer 7 sandwich 8 Wednesday 9 postcard 10 breakfast 11 vegetables 12 fruit 13 bread 14 chocolate

7A We're twins

1 2 animals 3 visiting new places 4 dancing 5 horror films 6 shopping for clothes 7 flying 8 classical music 9 watching sport on TV

2 1 I love 2 I like 3 I don't like 4 I hate

3 2 She **likes** classical music.
3 She **doesn't like** football.
4 She **hates** watching sport on TV.
5 Andy **loves** dancing.
6 He **likes** rock **music**.
7 He **doesn't** like tennis.
8 He **hates** horror **films**.
9 Andy and Mel **love** ice **cream**.
10 They **like** Chinese **food**.
11 They **don't like** coffee.
12 They **hate** flying.

4 2 him 3 them 4 her 5 it 6 us

5 2 I phone **him** every day. 3 **We** don't know **them**. 4 Do **they** know **her**? 5 **She** plays tennis with **me**. 6 **He** never talks to **us**.

6 2 Fiona **doesn't** work in an office.
3 Where **does** your daughter live?
4 Lin **studies** English at a language school in London.
5 What **do** your parents do in the evening?
6 Lydia and Pia **don't** like soap operas.
7 My brother **has** three cars.
8 Tom's son **works** for a computer company.
9 Jack **watches** TV every evening.
10 What time do you **start** work?

7B Can you drive?

1 1 swim 2 drive 3 sing 4 guitar 5 ride 6 piano 7 speak 8 ski 9 play 10 cook

2 2 They **can ski**. 3 Tamara **can't sing**. 4 She **can cook** very well. 5 They **can't speak** Russian.

3 2 Can your sister drive? Yes, she can. No, she can't. 3 Can your parents speak French? Yes, they can. No, they can't. 4 Can your son play the piano? Yes, he can. No, he can't. 5 Can you do this exercise? Yes, I can. (Yes, we can.) No, I can't. (No, we can't.)

Answer Key

4

places in a town or city	things in your bag	colours
theatre	keys	grey
station	credit card	red
park	map	white
square	money	pink
museum	passport	black

7C Directions

1 2 opposite 3 next to 4 in 5 on
6 near 7 opposite 8 next to

2 2 the chemist's 3 the bank
4 the hotel 5 the restaurant

3 2 Go along 3 That's 4 on the left
5 opposite 6 Is there 7 near here
8 turn left 9 on your right
10 next to

7D The internet

1 **download** videos, **listen** to the radio, **be** on Facebook, **watch** videos, **book** a holiday, **be** on Twitter, **get** or **receive** emails, **read** a blog, **book** a flight, **download** apps, **buy** DVDs online, **book** a hotel, **send** emails, **watch** TV programmes, **chat** to friends and family, **search** for information, **write** a blog, **download** photos, **listen** to music

2a 2 I send a lot of emails **every day**.
3 I **usually** buy concert tickets online.
4 I watch videos on YouTube **every week**. 5 I **always** book flights online.
6 I **sometimes** buy and sell things on eBay. 7 I chat to friends online **every weekend**. 8 I **never** watch TV programmes online. 9 I **don't usually** download music. 10 I get about twenty emails **every day**.

3b 2 shop 3 lesson 4 sugar 5 sure
6 she 7 Spanish

4 2 visiting 3 basketball 4 animals
5 different 6 usually 7 evening
8 passport 9 wallet 10 holiday

5 2 a jacket 3 a jumper 4 a shirt
5 trousers 6 a skirt 7 boots
8 shoes

8A I was there

1a 2 short 3 full 4 easy 5 right
6 young 7 happy 8 awful
9 fantastic

b 2 long 3 empty 4 difficult
5 wrong 6 old 7 unhappy
8 amazing 9 terrible

2 2 were, Athens 3 third, was
4 was, 30 5 were, films 6 was, the USA 7 100th, was 8 were, tennis players 9 was, Ronald Reagan 10 were, 4.8
11 were, footballers 12 were, 26

3 2 There weren't six people in The Beatles. There were four (people).
3 The 1998 World Cup wasn't in Spain. It was in France. 4 The 2000 Olympic Games weren't in London. They were in Sydney.
5 Elvis Presley wasn't British. He was American. 6 William Shakespeare wasn't from Australia. He was from the UK.

4 2 I **wasn't** at home on Friday. 3 You **aren't** in this class. / You're not in this class. 4 **There's** a bank in Park Road. 5 We **weren't** at the concert.
6 I'm sorry, she **isn't** here. / I'm sorry, **she's not** here. 7 They **don't** work at home. 8 He **doesn't** like pizza.

8B Happy anniversary!

1 b 1938 c 1963 d 1970 e 2003
f 2013

2a b He was in China four years **ago**.
c He was in Los Angeles **in** 2001.
d He was in Venice **yesterday**.
e He was in Australia **last** year.
f He was in London three days **ago**.

b 2 f 3 a 4 e 5 b 6 c

3 2 was 3 was 4 were 5 wasn't
6 weren't 7 were 8 was 9 was

4a 2 How old were they on their wedding day? 3 When was their golden wedding anniversary?
4 Where was the party? 5 How many people were at the party?
6 Where was Jean's brother?

b b 5 c 6 d 3 e 2 f 4

5 2 Was; Yes, it was. 3 Were; Yes, there were. 4 Was; No, he wasn't.
5 Were; No, they weren't. 6 Were; Yes, I was. / No, I wasn't. 7 Were; Yes, I was. / No, I wasn't. 8 Was; Yes, he was. / No, he wasn't.

6 1 I was born in (place).
2 were; I was born in (year).
3 was; She was born in (place).
4 was; He was born in (year).

7 2 on 3 to 4 on 5 to 6 in
7 on 8 in, in

8C Birthdays

1 2 February 3 March 4 April
5 May 6 June 7 July 8 August
9 September 10 October
11 November 12 December

2 1st first, 2nd second, 3rd third, 4th fourth, 5th fifth, 6th sixth, 7th seventh, 8th eighth, 9th ninth, 10th tenth, 12th twelfth, 15th fifteenth, 20th twentieth, 23rd twenty-third, 30th thirtieth, 31st thirty-first

3 **What** day **is** it today? It's Saturday.
What's the **date** today? May **the** thirteenth.
When's your birthday? It's **on** July the twenty-ninth.
What **day was** it yesterday? Friday.

4 1 b 2 e 3 d 4 f 5 c 6 g
7 a 8 h

5 2 What shall we 3 Why don't
4 Maybe 5 Let's go 6 a good idea
7 shall we 8 Let's meet
9 What time

8D Life's a party!

1a b 250 c 895 d 1,000 e 10,800
f 150,000 g 1,000,000
h 40,000,000

b b seven hundred and fifty c two thousand d seventeen thousand, five hundred e a / one hundred thousand
f eight million

2b 3 S 4 D 5 S 6 S 7 D 8 S
9 D 10 D

3 Across 1 passport 4 fish 7 coat
8 chicken 10 wallet 12 river
13 laptop 14 magazine 17 purse
18 chips 19 batteries 21 bread
23 guitar 24 dress 25 cheese
Down 2 suit 3 pencil 5 ice cream
6 postcard 9 tie 10 watch
11 trainers 15 eggs 16 bike
20 T-shirt 21 burger 22 apple

9A Amazing journeys

1 2 a boat 3 a bus 4 a plane
5 a bike 6 a train 7 a motorbike
8 a taxi

2 2 wanted 3 arrived 4 visited
5 studied 6 travelled 7 started
8 finished 9 cooked 10 listened
11 walked 12 played 13 looked
14 hated 15 asked 16 helped
17 chatted 18 booked 19 lived
20 watched

Answer Key

3a

```
Y L C O M E F V
W G S D Q G O S
E I D E T E L L
B V I L P Q P E
U E C X K Y T A
Y O T I G M L V
E F H A V E C E
G E T I X E A M
H J W R I T E U
```

b go → went, tell → told, have → had, get → got, write → wrote, buy → bought, give → gave, meet → met, leave → left

4a 2 got 3 left 4 had 5 wrote 6 went 7 met 8 bought 9 gave 10 told

5 2 started 3 walked 4 went 5 left 6 arrived 7 walked 8 finished 9 travelled 10 raised 11 wrote

9B My last holiday

1 2 **go on** holiday 3 **take** photos 4 **go** swimming 5 **stay in** a hotel 6 **go for** a walk 7 **stay with** friends or family 8 **travel** around 9 **go** sightseeing 10 **go to** the beach 11 **rent** a car

2 2 stayed 3 rented 4 travelled 5 went 6 didn't go 7 had 8 didn't stay 9 had 10 went 11 didn't stay 12 stayed 13 went 14 didn't take 15 didn't have 16 had 17 met 18 didn't want

3a 2 What did they do in the afternoons?
3 Where did they have dinner?
4 When did Jeremy go to Prague?
5 Who did he stay with?
6 What did he do in the mornings?

b a 6 b 1 c 3 d 5 e 4 f 2

4a 2 Did they go to the beach every day?
3 Did they go to any clubs?
4 Did Jeremy take any photos?
5 Did he like Prague Castle?
6 Did he meet any nice people?

b 2 Yes, they did. 3 No, they didn't. 4 No, he didn't. 5 Yes, he did. 6 Yes, he did.

9C A weekend away

1 a return 6, a customer 4, a ticket machine 2, a single 5, a platform 3

2 2 Next Saturday.
3 Thanks. What time's the next train?
4 Which platform?
5 What time does it arrive in Leeds?
6 Thanks a lot. Bye.

3a 2 What did you do at the weekend?
3 Did you have a good time?
4 What did you do there?
5 Where did you go?
6 What did you see?
7 Did you enjoy it?

b 2 What did you see?
3 Did you enjoy it?
4 What did you do at the weekend?
5 Where did you go?
6 What did you do there?
7 Did you have a good time?

9D Who, what, when?

1 1 What, c 2 How many, b 3 When, b 4 Who, a 5 How old, b 6 Where, c 7 How much, b 8 Why, a

2

/tʃ/	/dʒ/
cheese	oran**ge** **j**uice
chips	**j**acket
chicken	**j**ob
sandwi**ch**	mana**g**er

/s/	/ʃ/
suit	**sh**irt
sell	**sh**op
city	**s**ugar
le**ss**on	Briti**sh**

/ɔː/	/ɜː/
f**or**ty	b**ur**ger
sp**or**t	f**ir**st
f**our**	w**or**k
August	**ear**ly

3 2 guitar 3 wrong 4 friends 5 interesting 6 different 7 young 8 guide book 9 wrote 10 school 11 centre 12 people 13 grandfather 14 daughter

10A Life changes

1
- start — school or university / a **new** job
- leave — school or **university** / your job
- do — a (computer) **course** / an **exam**
- move — **house** / to another **city** or country
- get — **engaged** / married
- look for — a house or a **flat** / a (new) job

2 1 a 2 h 3 c 4 f 5 g 6 e 7 b 8 d

3 2 'm not going to look for 3 are going to travel 4 aren't going to drive / 're not going to drive 5 're going to go ('re going) 6 are going to move 7 'm going to start 8 isn't going to look for / 's not going to look for 9 's going to write 10 are going to get 11 aren't going to have / 're not going to have 12 're going to go ('re going)

4 2 I **don't** like shopping for clothes. 3 My parents **aren't** going to move house. 4 I **didn't** go out with friends last night. 5 Katherine **doesn't** work at home. 6 There **isn't** a station near my flat. 7 I **can't** play the piano. 8 Lisa and Zak **don't have** a dog.

5a 2 were 3 did 4 was 5 did 6 was 7 were 8 did

b a 7 b 4 c 3 d 1 e 2 f 8 g 6 h 5

10B A new start

1 2 have dinner with friends 3 go running 4 watch the news 5 go swimming 6 go to the cinema 7 go to the gym 8 go shopping 9 watch sport on TV 10 have coffee with friends 11 have a party 12 go to a party

2 2 Where **are** you **going** to stay? 3 What **are** you **going to** do next weekend? 4 What **are you going to** buy? 5 What **are** you **going to** do after the course? 6 **What's** she **going to do**? 7 **Where's she going to** study?

3a 2 Are they going to stay in a hotel? 3 Is Lucy going to go shopping on Saturday? 4 Is she going to buy a new laptop? 5 Is Hugo going to look for a job? 6 Is Laura going to do a German course?

b 2 No, they aren't. / No, they're not. 3 Yes, she is. 4 No, she isn't. 5 Yes, he is. 6 No, she isn't.

4a 2 a 3 e 4 g 5 h 6 b 7 d 8 f

b 2 No, he isn't. / No, he's not. 3 No, I don't. 4 No, he doesn't. 5 No, I can't. 6 No, there isn't. 7 No, there aren't. 8 No, I didn't.

10C Good luck!

1 2 excited 3 happy 4 scared 5 tired 6 bored 7 hungry 8 angry

2 2 a lot 3 See you in 4 Yes, see you 5 Have a good 6 good luck with 7 very much 8 See you

Answer Key

3
dancing	**four**teenth
happy	nineteenth
boring	guitar
April	July
yesterday	Sep**tem**ber
difficult	fantastic
animals	amazing
basketball	December

4 2 gave 3 came 4 bought 5 met
6 wrote 7 went 8 left 9 had
10 got

Reading and Writing Portfolio 1

1 3 a 4 d 5 c 6 e
3a 2 Where are you from? 3 My name's William. 4 Where's she from? 5 I'm from the UK. 6 How are you? 7 She's from the USA. 8 I'm fine, thanks.
  b question 2 → answer 5, question 4 → answer 7, question 6 → answer 8
5 2 Luciano's from Italy. 3 Where's Elizabeth from? 4 Alexei's from Moscow. 5 Hello, I'm David Smith. 6 Nick's from Bristol, in the UK. 7 She's from Orlando, in the USA.
6 1 A What's your first name?
     B It's Abdul.
     A What's your surname?
     B It's Razzaq.
   2 A Where are you from?
     B I'm from Brazil. And you?
     A I'm from Izmir, in Turkey.
     B Nice to meet you.
     A You too.
7a Students' answers
  b 2 My surname's … . 3 I'm from … .
    4 My mobile number's … .
    5 My home number's … .

Reading and Writing Portfolio 2

1 1C 2A 3B
2 2 He's from **Sydney**. 3 His email address is **s.davis@gmail.net**.
4 Janet Richards is **American**.
5 She's **a manager**. 6 Her phone number is **206 818 7904**. 7 Lucy Smith is **an actress**. 8 She's **British**.
9 Her **mobile** number is 07986 342187.
4b 2 Is Benetton an Italian company?
3 Her name is Mrs Alice Roberts.
4 Are you Mr Henry Long? 5 Ford is an American company. 6 Her address is 1306 South Beach, Miami.
7 My address is 26 New Street, London SW19 4GP.

5

PH PARK HOTEL

Registration form
first name Lucy
surname Smith
nationality British
address 76 Queen Street, Manchester
postcode M18 3JS
home number 0161 284 9865
mobile number 07986 342187
email address lucy.smith@webmail.co.uk
room number 617

Reading and Writing Portfolio 3

1b 2 b 3 a 4 b 5 b 6 a 7 b
3 2 I'm an actor and she's a teacher.
3 You're Sally's brother. 4 They aren't Bob's children. 5 We're in Mr West's English class. 6 They're French and he's Italian. 7 What's your father's name? 8 Where's Jack's wife from? 9 Mary's mother isn't from the UK. 10 Who's Helena's English teacher?
5 2 Our hotel is very cheap, but it isn't near the beach. 3 The restaurant is nice and the food is very good.
4 I love fruit and I eat a lot of vegetables. 5 She's a German teacher, but she isn't from Germany.
6 They're my friends, but they aren't in my class. 7 Simon's my son and Yvonne's my daughter. 8 Brian is friendly, but his brother is very unfriendly. 9 She's from London and she's an actress.
6 1 and 2 but 3 but 4 and

Reading and Writing Portfolio 4

1 3 He's **single**. 4 ✓ 5 **Four** people live in his flat. 6 Sam and Pat are Danny's **brothers**. 7 ✓
3 2 I work in a very big office.
3 My grandparents have a new car.
4 My wife and I don't go to concerts.
5 I live in a very small flat. 6 Our children study languages in London.
4a 1 I live <u>in</u> a big flat <u>in</u> Notting Hill with three friends.
2 I work <u>for</u> a TV company <u>in</u> the centre of London.
3 I study Spanish <u>at</u> a language school.

5 2 the centre of 3 hotel 4 have a son 5 tennis 6 to the cinema
7 a language school 8 my children

Reading and Writing Portfolio 5

1b 2 She **isn't** married. 3 She's a **music** journalist. 4 She's **a singer** in a rock band. 5 She goes **to the cinema** in her free time. 6 She **doesn't eat** chicken. 7 She **sometimes** has Italian food. 8 She **likes** coffee.
9 Juliet **doesn't live** in Dublin.
10 Juliet **always** sees Katie on her birthday.
4 2 and 3 because 4 but 5 because
6 but 7 because 8 and
5 2 That car is beautiful. It's **also** very expensive. 3 She has three cats. She **also** has a dog. 4 Kevin's an actor. He's **also** a musician. 5 Gina loves lasagne. She **also** likes pizza.
6 2 and 3 and 4 also 5 because
6 and 7 but 8 also 9 because
10 also

Reading and Writing Portfolio 6

1b 2 £37.80 3 Waterloo. 4 Yes, there are. 5 Yes, it is. 6 No, it isn't.
7 Yes, it is. 8 Yes, there are.
9 Yes, there are.
3 2 very popular with 3 a great place to 4 you can also 5 There are 6 is open from 7 very popular with 8 You can 9 a great place to 10 There's also 11 there are
12 every day
4 2 T 3 F 4 F 5 T 6 T

Reading and Writing Portfolio 7

1b 2 T 3 T 4 F 5 F 6 F 7 T 8 F
3 2 Tom doesn't like dogs, but I love **them**. 3 Anna's my best friend and I email **her** every day. 4 I love rock music, but my sister doesn't like **it**.
5 Pete's my son and I love **him** very much. 6 I love horror films, but my wife hates **them**.
6 My daughter's name is Daisy and we **both** like a lot of the same things. We **both** love clothes and sometimes go shopping **together**. And we **both** love black and white films. On Sunday afternoons we **usually** watch an old film **together**. With a big box of chocolates, of course!

Answer Key

Daisy and I are also very different. She doesn't like flying, but I love **it**. And I like soap operas, but Daisy hates **them**. I watch two soap operas **every evening**. Daisy also loves cooking, but I hate **it**. In our home my husband cooks dinner **every day**! I think Daisy is the best daughter in the world and I love **her** very much.

7 They both love clothes, shopping, black and white films, and chocolates.

Reading and Writing Portfolio 8

1a 1 c 2 a 3 b 4 d
 b 2 0844 782 1176
   3 At the City Theatre
   4 At www.thecitytheatre.co.uk.
   5 At the Apollo Cinema.
   6 Julia Ross
   7 At 7.30 p.m.
   8 £30, £25 and £20
2 She was at a Big Noise concert at the Birmingham Arena.
4 2 a 3 a 4 the 5 the 6 a 7 The 8 the 9 a 10 the 11 The 12 the

Reading and Writing Portfolio 9

1b 1 C 2 B 3 A
  c 2 went sightseeing 3 near 4 Ollie 5 Friday 6 Isla Holbox
4 2 I was very tired so I went to bed early. (I went to bed early because I was very tired.) 3 When we arrived in Paris, we went for a walk. (We went for a walk when we arrived in Paris.) 4 He went by train because he hates flying. (He hates flying so he went by train.) 5 When I got home, I phoned my sister. (I phoned my sister when I got home.) 6 There weren't any taxis so we rented a car. (We rented a car because there weren't any taxis.)
5a She went to Bordeaux, in France. She had a good time.
  b 2 so 3 When 4 and 5 because 6 so 7 and 8 because 9 but 10 because 11 When

Reading and Writing Portfolio 10

1 1 B 2 A 3 C
3 2 Happy 3 Have 4 day 5 love 6 To 7 luck 8 your 9 wishes 10 on 11 new 12 soon 13 Love

5 Dear Beth
Thank you very much for your birthday card and the present. It's a beautiful watch and I wear it **every day**.
I had a very nice birthday **on Saturday**. I met my sister in town and we went shopping **together**. I **also** went to a concert with Eddie **in the evening**. The concert was fantastic and we **both** had a great time.
Life in London is very good. I have a new job **with a TV company**. I love the job, but **I never** get home before 8 p.m. Eddie is **also** very busy. We're **always** very tired, but we're very happy **together**. Did you know that we got engaged **last month**? We're going to get married **next July**!
Lots of love Diana

6 1 Her sister. 2 They went to a concert. 3 Last month. 4 Next July.

VOCABULARY AND SKILLS
7D The internet

Things people do online VOCABULARY 7.5

1 Match the verbs in A to the words or phrases in B.

A	B
sell	videos
download	things online
listen	on Facebook
be	to the radio

watch | on Twitter
book | emails
be | a holiday
get / receive | videos

read | a flight
book | apps
download | DVDs online
buy | a blog

book | a hotel
send | TV programmes
watch | emails
chat | to friends and family

search | a blog
write | to music
download | for information
listen | photos

Review: frequency adverbs and phrases with *every*

2 a Put the words in brackets ( ) in the correct place in these sentences.

never
1 I ⟋ listen to the radio online. (never)
2 I send a lot of emails. (every day)
3 I buy concert tickets online. (usually)
4 I watch videos on YouTube. (every week)
5 I book flights online. (always)
6 I buy and sell things on eBay. (sometimes)
7 I chat to friends online. (every weekend)
8 I watch TV programmes online. (never)
9 I download music. (don't usually)
10 I get about twenty emails. (every day)

b Tick the sentences in **2a** that are true for you.

Pronunciation: /s/ and /ʃ/
HELP WITH PRONUNCIATION Student's Book p61

3 a Look at these pictures. Check you remember the sounds /s/ and /ʃ/.

/s/ suit   /ʃ/ shirt

b Look at the consonants in **bold**. Which sound is different?

1 (suit) shirt Spanish   5 sure   skirt   small
2 shop   city   expensive   6 police pencil she
3 Russian tissues lesson   7 Egyptian Spanish
4 sell   sugar centre   Turkish

Spelling: double letters (2)

4 S Circle the words with the correct spelling.

1 shoping / (shopping)   6 usualy / usually
2 visiting / visitting   7 evening / evenning
3 basketbal / basketball   8 pasport / passport
4 animals / animmals   9 walet / wallet
5 diferent / different   10 holiday / holliday

Spelling: clothes

5 S Look at the shopping website. Write the words.

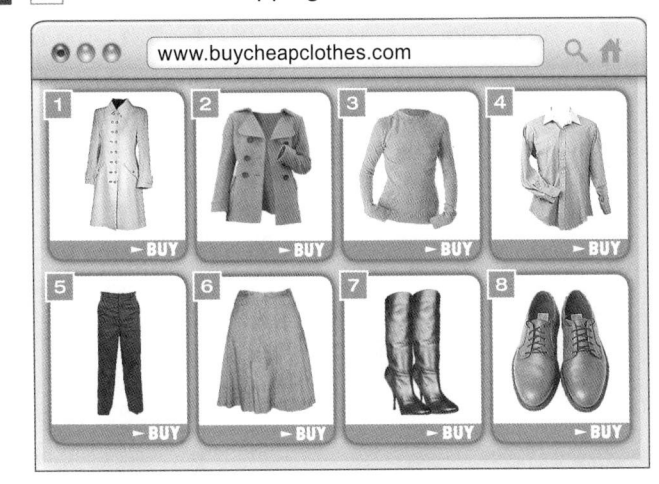

www.buycheapclothes.com

1 a c *oat*   5 t_____
2 a j_____   6 a s_____
3 a j_____   7 b_____
4 a s_____   8 s_____

Reading and Writing Portfolio 7 p64

37

8A I was there

Language Summary 8, Student's Book p128

Adjectives (2) VOCABULARY 8.1

1 a S Find the adjectives.

```
1  F  E  S  W (B  O  R  I  N  G) R  G  W  K
2  L  O  P  R  Y  I  S  H  O  R  T  A  W  Q
3  A  L  P  I  Q  F  U  L  L  E  A  S  P  U
4  N  E  V  A  U  R  F  D  E  A  S  Y  G  E
5  P  A  R  I  G  R  I  G  H  T  W  O  U  J
6  T  O  M  O  N  A  I  Z  Y  O  U  N  G  P
7  V  A  H  A  P  P  Y  A  P  O  N  O  R  C
8  S  T  E  B  R  A  N  A  W  F  U  L  E  Y
9  A  V  F  A  N  T  A  S  T  I  C  I  L  P
```

b Write the opposites of the adjectives in **1a**.

1 i _n t e r e s t i n g_
2 l _ _ _ _
3 e _ _ _ _ _ _ _
4 d _ _ _ _ _ _ _ _
5 w _ _ _ _ _
6 o _ _ _
7 u _ _ _ _ _ _ _
8 a _ _ _ z _ _ _ _
9 t _ _ _ _ _ b _ _

Past Simple of be: positive and negative GRAMMAR 8.1

2 Fill in the gaps with *was* or *were*. Then choose the correct answers.

Those were the days!

In 2004 ...

1 The British Prime Minister ___was___ Margaret Thatcher / (Tony Blair) / David Cameron.
2 The Olympic Games _____ in Sydney / Athens / Beijing.
3 The *first / third / fifth* Harry Potter film _____ in cinemas.
4 The actor Leonardo DiCaprio _____ 20 / 30 / 40 years old.

Leonardo DiCaprio

In 1994 ...

5 *Forrest Gump* and *The Lion King* _____ new *films / TV programmes / books*.
6 The football World Cup _____ in *Brazil / the USA / France*.
7 The *1st / 100th / 300th* episode of *The Simpsons* _____ on TV.
8 Steffi Graf and Martina Navratilova _____ famous *musicians / tennis players / actresses*.

Steffi Graf

In 1984 ...

9 The President of the USA _____ John F Kennedy / Jimmy Carter / Ronald Reagan.
10 There _____ 3.8 / 4.8 / 5.8 billion* people in the world.
11 Diego Maradona and Michel Platini _____ famous *tennis players / footballers / actors*.
12 The singers Madonna and Prince _____ 16 / 26 / 36 years old.

Madonna

*a billion = 1,000,000,000

3 Make these sentences negative. Write the correct sentences. Use the words in brackets.

1 The last Beatles concert was in the UK. (the USA)
  The last Beatles concert wasn't in the UK.
  It was in the USA.

2 There were six people in The Beatles. (four)

3 The 1998 World Cup was in Spain. (France)

4 The 2000 Olympic Games were in London. (Sydney)

5 Elvis Presley was British. (American)

6 William Shakespeare was from Australia. (the UK)

Review: contractions (2)

4 Write these sentences with contractions (*I'm*, *aren't*, etc.).

1 They are from Colombia.
  They're from Colombia.

2 I was not at home on Friday.

3 You are not in this class.

4 There is a bank in Park Road.

5 We were not at the concert.

6 I am sorry, she is not here.

7 They do not work at home.

8 He does not like pizza.

8B Happy anniversary!

Years and past time phrases VOCABULARY 8.2

1 Match these years to the words.

~~1790~~ 2013 1970 1938 1963 2003

seventeen ninety — a *1790*

nineteen thirty-eight — b _____

nineteen sixty-three — c _____

nineteen seventy — d _____

two thousand and three — e _____

twenty thirteen — f _____

2 a Fill in the gaps with *yesterday*, *in*, *last* and *ago*.

a Leon was in Japan *last* month.
b He was in China four years _____ .
c He was in Los Angeles _____ 2001.
d He was in Venice _____ .
e He was in Australia _____ year.
f He was in London three days _____ .

b Put pictures a–f in order from now.

1 *d* 2 ___ 3 ___ 4 ___ 5 ___ 6 ___

Review: Past Simple of *be*

3 Read about Frank and Jean's wedding anniversary. Fill in the gaps with *was*, *were*, *wasn't* or *weren't*.

Frank and I ¹ _were_ (+) both 23 on our wedding day, and last Sunday it ² _____ (+) our golden wedding anniversary*. There ³ _____ (+) a big party at a hotel and about a hundred people ⁴ _____ (+) there. My brother ⁵ _____ (−) at the party because he was in Australia. Also Frank's two sisters ⁶ _____ (−) there. They're both very old and can't travel. But our two sons and their families ⁷ _____ (+) at the party. The food ⁸ _____ (+) fantastic and it ⁹ _____ (+) one of the best days of our lives.

*golden wedding anniversary = married for 50 years

Past Simple of *be*: questions and short answers; *was born / were born* GRAMMAR 8.2

4 a Make questions with these words.

1 Frank and Jean's / was / wedding / When ?
   When was Frank and Jean's wedding?
2 they / on / were / their wedding day / How old ?
   _____
3 When / golden wedding anniversary / their / was ?
   _____
4 party / Where / was / the ?
   _____
5 people / the party / How many / at / were ?
   _____
6 was / brother / Jean's / Where ?
   _____

b Match the questions in **4a** to these answers.

a Fifty years ago. _1_   d Last Sunday. ____
b About a hundred. ____ e They were both 23. ____
c He was in Australia. ____ f At a hotel. ____

5 Choose the correct words in these questions. Then write the short answers.

1 *Was* / (*Were*) Frank and Jean married 50 years ago?
   Yes, _they were._
2 *Was* / *Were* their anniversary party at a hotel?
   _____
3 *Was* / *Were* there a lot of people at the party?
   _____
4 *Was* / *Were* Jean's brother at the party?
   _____
5 *Was* / *Were* Frank's sisters at the party?
   _____
6 *Was* / *Were* you at home last night?
   _____
7 *Was* / *Were* you in Australia last week?
   _____
8 *Was* / *Were* your father born in Spain?
   _____

6 Fill in the gaps in questions 1–4 with *was* or *were*. Then write your answers.

1 Where _were_ you born?
   I was born _____.
2 When _____ you born?
   I was _____.
3 Where _____ your mother born?
   She _____.
4 When _____ your father born?
   He _____.

Review: prepositions (2)

7 Choose the correct prepositions.

1 I don't work *to* / (*at*) the weekend.
2 The post office is *in* / *on* the left.
3 I never listen *to* / *for* the radio.
4 Do you watch sport *on* / *in* TV?
5 The café is next *of* / *to* the bank.
6 I play tennis *on* / *in* the morning.
7 I get up late *on* / *in* Sunday mornings.
8 I was born *in* / *on* Italy *at* / *in* 1987.

8C REAL WORLD Birthdays

Months and dates VOCABULARY 8.3

1 S Write the letters in the months.

1 J a n u a ry
2 F _ br _ _ ry
3 M _ _ c _
4 Ap _ _ l
5 M _ _
6 J _ _ e
7 J _ _ y
8 A _ g _ _ t
9 S _ pt _ _ b _ r
10 O _ _ ob _ r
11 N _ v _ _ be _
12 D _ _ e _ _ er

2 Match the dates to the words.

eighth   12th   fifteenth
1st — first   tenth   third
6th   23rd   30th
twentieth   fifth   20th
7th   2nd   sixth   8th
twelfth   9th   thirtieth
10th   5th
   fourth   ninth
second   31st   15th
4th
   thirty-first   seventh
twenty-third   3rd

Talking about days and dates
REAL WORLD 8.1

3 Fill in the gaps with these words.

| What | When's | What's | date |
| day | was | is | the | on |

What day it today? — It's Saturday.

____ the ____ today? — May thirteenth.

____ your birthday? — It's ____ July the twenty-ninth.

What ____ it yesterday? — Friday.

Making suggestions REAL WORLD 8.2

4 Put the conversation in order.

Colin   Ruth

COLIN
a OK. What time shall we meet?
b What shall we do this evening? 1
c Yes, that's a good idea. Where shall we meet?
d No, I don't think so. We went to the theatre last month.

RUTH
e Why don't we go to the theatre?
f OK. Let's go to that Japanese restaurant.
g Let's meet at the restaurant. It's in West Street.
h About half past seven. 8

5 Fill in the gaps in this conversation with these phrases.

Poppy   Toshi

| How are you | Let's meet | Let's go | What shall we |
| shall we | What time | a good idea | Why don't | Maybe |

POPPY Hi, Toshi.
TOSHI Hello, Poppy. ¹ _How are you_ ?
POPPY I'm fine, thanks. ² _____ do today?
TOSHI ³ _____ we go to the park?
POPPY ⁴ _____ . But we always go to the park.
TOSHI OK. ⁵ _____ to the museum.
POPPY Yes, that's ⁶ _____ .
       Where ⁷ _____ meet?
TOSHI ⁸ _____ at the station.
POPPY OK. ⁹ _____ shall we meet?
TOSHI At about one o'clock. Then we can have lunch first.
POPPY Great! See you then. Bye.

41

VOCABULARY AND SKILLS 8D — Life's a party!

Big numbers VOCABULARY 8.4

1 a Write the numbers.

a a hundred *100*
b two hundred and fifty _____
c eight hundred and ninety-five _____
d a thousand _____
e ten thousand, eight hundred _____
f a hundred and fifty thousand _____
g a million _____
h forty million _____

b Write the numbers in words.

a 100 *a hundred*
b 750 _____
c 2,000 _____
d 17,500 _____
e 100,000 _____
f 8,000,000 _____

Pronunciation: /ɔː/ and /ɜː/

HELP WITH PRONUNCIATION Student's Book p69

2 a Look at these pictures. Check you remember the sounds /ɔː/ and /ɜː/.

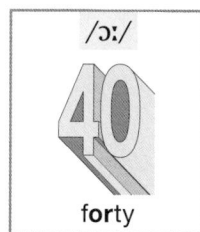

/ɔː/ f**or**ty
/ɜː/ b**ur**ger

b Look at the letters in **bold**. Are the letter sounds the same (S) or different (D)?

1 sh**ir**t sk**ir**t S
2 **ear**ly **Au**gust D
3 w**a**ter d**augh**ter
4 f**our** s**ur**name
5 f**ir**st w**or**k
6 m**or**ning **aw**ful
7 sm**all** g**ir**l
8 G**er**man th**ir**ty
9 **a**lways T**ur**kish
10 sh**or**t th**ir**d

Spelling: review

3 S Do the crossword.

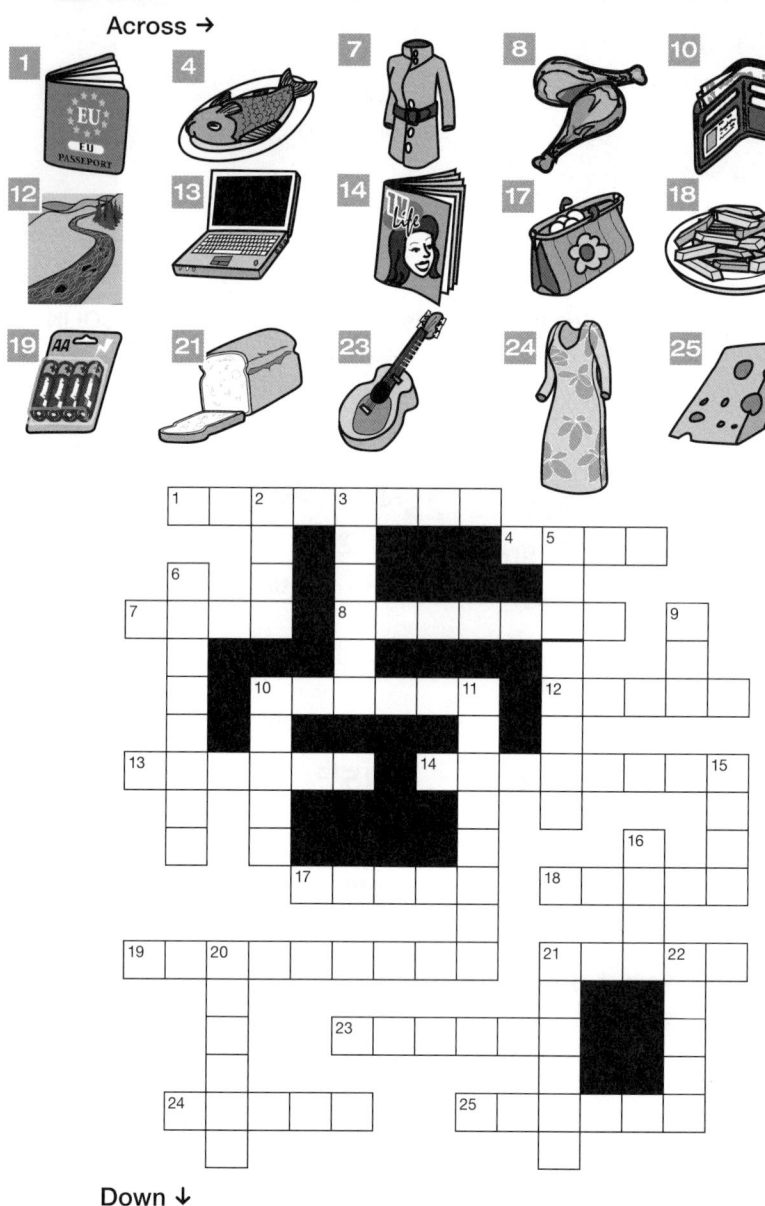

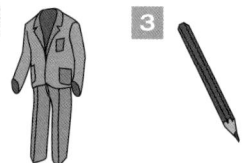

Across →

Down ↓

Reading and Writing Portfolio 8 p66

9A Amazing journeys

Language Summary 9, Student's Book p130

Transport VOCABULARY 9.1

1 [S] Write the words.

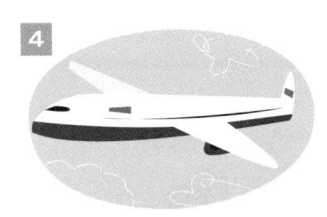

1 a c _a r_
2 a b _ _ _ _
3 a b _ _ _
4 a p _ _ _ _ _
5 a b _ _ _ _
6 a t _ _ _ _ _
7 a m _ _ _ _ _ _ _ _
8 a t _ _ _ _

Past Simple: positive (regular verbs)
GRAMMAR 9.1

2 Write the Past Simple forms of these regular verbs.

1	like	_liked_	11	walk
2	want		12	play
3	arrive		13	look
4	visit		14	hate
5	study		15	ask
6	travel		16	help
7	start		17	chat
8	finish		18	book
9	cook		19	live
10	listen		20	watch

Past Simple: positive (irregular verbs)
GRAMMAR 9.1

3 a Find ten irregular verbs (→ ↓).

Y	L	C	O	M	E	F	V
W	G	S	D	Q	G	O	S
E	I	D	E	T	E	L	L
B	V	I	L	P	Q	P	E
U	E	C	X	K	Y	T	A
Y	O	T	I	G	M	L	V
E	F	H	A	V	E	C	E
G	E	T	I	X	E	A	M
H	J	W	R	I	T	E	U

b Write the verbs in **3a** and their Past Simple forms.

come → _came_
_____ → _____
_____ → _____
_____ → _____
_____ → _____
_____ → _____
_____ → _____
_____ → _____
_____ → _____
_____ → _____

4 a Fill in the gaps with the irregular Past Simple forms in **3b**.

1 I _came_ home by bus yesterday.
2 I _____ up at 7.00 yesterday morning.
3 I _____ home at 8.00 yesterday morning.
4 I _____ dinner at 8.30 last night.
5 I _____ an email to a friend yesterday.
6 I _____ to the cinema last weekend.
7 I _____ some friends in a café last weekend.
8 I _____ some new clothes last month.
9 My parents _____ me some money for my last birthday.
10 My teacher _____ me to learn my irregular verbs!

b Tick (✓) the sentences in **4a** that are true for you.

5 Read about Ffyona Campbell's journey. Fill in the gaps with the Past Simple of the verbs in brackets ( ).

Ffyona's long walk

Ffyona Campbell [1] _was_ (be) the first woman to walk around the world. She [2] _____ (start) her journey in the UK in 1983 and then in 1985 she [3] _____ (walk) across the USA. In 1988 she [4] _____ (go) from Sydney to Perth in only 95 days. On 2nd April 1991, Ffyona [5] _____ (leave) Cape Town in South Africa. She [6] _____ (arrive) in Morocco 29 months later – a journey of 10,000 miles. Then she [7] _____ (walk) across Europe and [8] _____ (finish) her journey in October 1994. She [9] _____ (travel) 19,586 miles and [10] _____ (raise) £120,000 for charity. Ffyona also [11] _____ (write) a book about her journey called _The Whole Story_.

9B My last holiday

Holiday activities VOCABULARY 9.2

1 Fill in the gaps in phrases 1–11 with these words.

~~have~~	rent	take	travel
stay in	stay with	go on
go for	go to	go (x2)

1 _have_ a good time
2 _____ holiday
3 _____ photos
4 _____ swimming
5 _____ a hotel
6 _____ a walk
7 _____ friends or family
8 _____ around
9 _____ sightseeing
10 _____ the beach
11 _____ a car

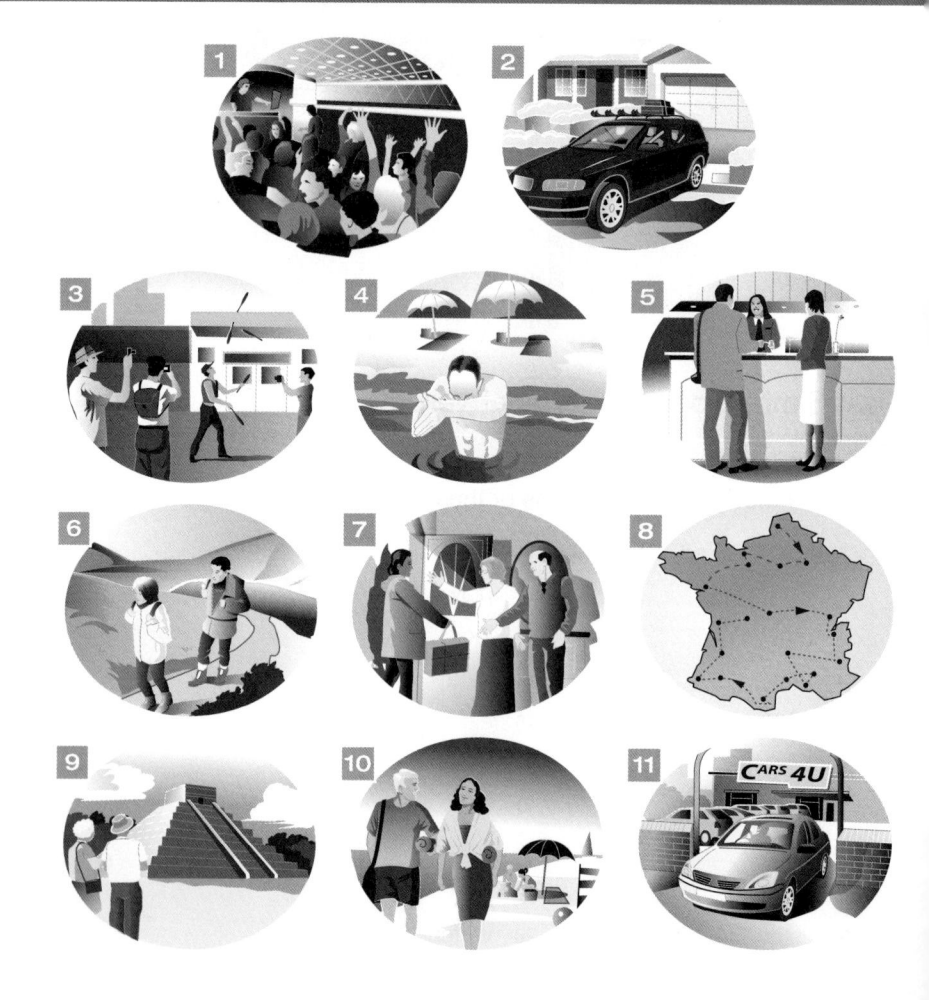

Past Simple: negative GRAMMAR 9.2

2 Read about these people's holidays. Put the verbs in the Past Simple.

Sandy and Naomi

Two years ago Sandy and I ¹ _went_ (go) on holiday to Ibiza, a beautiful Spanish island. We ² _____ (stay) in a very nice hotel near Ibiza Town. We ³ _____ (rent) a car and ⁴ _____ (travel) around the island – the scenery is amazing! We ⁵ _____ (go) to the beach every afternoon, but we ⁶ _____ (not go) to any clubs. And every evening we ⁷ _____ (have) dinner in Dalt Vila, the old part of Ibiza Town. Sandy and I ⁸ _____ (not stay) on the island very long, but we ⁹ _____ (have) a fantastic time!

Jeremy

Last August I ¹⁰ _____ (go) on holiday to Prague, in the Czech Republic. I ¹¹ _____ (not stay) in a hotel, I ¹² _____ (stay) with my friend Paul – he's a teacher there. I ¹³ _____ (go) sightseeing every morning, but I ¹⁴ _____ (not take) any photos because I ¹⁵ _____ (not have) my camera with me. My favourite place was Prague Castle – it's amazing! I ¹⁶ _____ (have) a great time in Prague and I ¹⁷ _____ (meet) some very nice people there. I ¹⁸ _____ (not want) to come home!

Past Simple: questions and short answers
GRAMMAR 9.3

3 a Make questions with these words.

1 Ibiza / Sandy and Naomi / did / to / When / go ?
   When did Sandy and Naomi go to Ibiza?

2 the afternoons / do / they / What / did / in ?
   _____

3 they / dinner / have / did / Where ?
   _____

4 Jeremy / did / When / to / Prague / go ?
   _____

5 with / Who / he / did / stay ?
   _____

6 did / the mornings / do / in / he / What ?
   _____

b Read about the people's holidays again in **2**. Then match answers a–f to questions 1–6 in **3a**.

a He went sightseeing.
b Two years ago. *1*
c In Dalt Vila.
d With his friend Paul.
e Last August.
f They went to the beach.

4 a Fill in the gaps with *Did* and these verbs.

| ~~rent~~ | like | meet | take | go (x2) |

1 _Did_ Sandy and Naomi _rent_ a car?
2 _____ they _____ to the beach every day?
3 _____ they _____ to any clubs?
4 _____ Jeremy _____ any photos?
5 _____ he _____ Prague Castle?
6 _____ he _____ any nice people?

b Write the short answers for the questions in **4a**.

1 _Yes, they did._
2 _____
3 _____
4 _____
5 _____
6 _____

9C REAL WORLD | A weekend away

At the station — VOCABULARY 9.3

1 Match these words to pictures 1–6.

- a ticket office **1**
- a return ☐
- a customer ☐
- a ticket machine ☐
- a single ☐
- a platform ☐

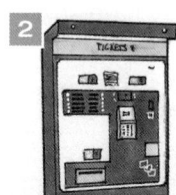

Buying train tickets — REAL WORLD 9.1

2 Pauline wants to buy a train ticket. Complete the conversation with these sentences.

> ~~A return to Leeds, please.~~   Which platform?
> Thanks. What time's the next train?   Next Saturday.
> What time does it arrive in Leeds?   Thanks a lot. Bye.

PAULINE   [1] *A return to Leeds, please.*
TICKET SELLER   When do you want to come back?
PAULINE   [2] _____
TICKET SELLER   That's £57.40, please. Here's your ticket.
PAULINE   [3] _____
TICKET SELLER   There's one at 10.15.
PAULINE   [4] _____
TICKET SELLER   Platform 1.
PAULINE   [5] _____
TICKET SELLER   At 12.48.
PAULINE   [6] _____

Asking about last weekend — REAL WORLD 9.2

3 a Make questions with these words.

1 have / weekend / Did / good / you / a ?
   Did you have a good weekend?
2 did / the / you / weekend / What / at / do ?
   _____
3 good / a / Did / time / have / you ?
   _____
4 there / What / do / you / did ?
   _____
5 you / did / go / Where ?
   _____
6 did / see / you / What ?
   _____
7 it / enjoy / you / Did ?
   _____

b Look at the photo and read the conversation. Then fill in the gaps with the questions from **3a**.

ROGER   Hi, Molly. [1] *Did you have a good weekend?*
MOLLY   Yes, I did, thanks. My husband and I went to the theatre on Saturday.
ROGER   Oh, nice. [2] _____
MOLLY   A play called *One of Those Days*.
ROGER   [3] _____
MOLLY   Yes, it was very good. And what about you? [4] _____
ROGER   I went away for the weekend.
MOLLY   Oh great! [5] _____
ROGER   I went to Cambridge to see some old friends.
MOLLY   [6] _____
ROGER   Well, on Saturday we went on the river and in the evening we all went out for dinner.
MOLLY   [7] _____
ROGER   Yes, I did, thanks. It was a great weekend.

9D VOCABULARY AND SKILLS
Who, what, when?

Question words VOCABULARY 9.4

1 Look at the quiz. Fill in the gaps with these words. Then choose the correct answers.

> When   What   How old   Where
> How much   Why   How many   Who

OUR WORLD

1 _____ is the capital of Brazil?
 a São Paulo.
 b Rio de Janeiro.
 c Brasília.

2 _____ countries are there in the world?
 a About 150.
 b About 200.
 c About 250.

3 _____ did the Berlin Wall come down?
 a In 1979.
 b In 1989.
 c In 1999.

4 _____ was the first President of the USA?
 a George Washington.
 b Thomas Jefferson.
 c John Adams.

5 _____ was John Lennon when he died in 1980?
 a He was 30.
 b He was 40.
 c He was 50.

6 _____ was the artist Pablo Picasso born?
 a In Venice, Italy.
 b In Paris, France.
 c In Málaga, Spain.

7 _____ were the first TVs in 1930?
 a About £8.
 b About £18.
 c About £80.

8 _____ don't many people live in Antarctica?
 a Because it's very cold.
 b Because it's very hot.
 c Because it's very expensive.

Pronunciation: sounds review (2)

HELP WITH PRONUNCIATION
Student's Book p53, p61, p69

2 Look at the letters in **bold** in these words. Write the words in the table.

> ~~ch~~ips   jacket   shop   sell   first
> sport   city   chicken   sugar   four
> job   work   manager   sandwich
> lesson   August   early   British

/tʃ/	/dʒ/
cheese	oran**ge** **j**uice
chips	

/s/	/ʃ/
suit	**sh**irt

/ɔː/	/ɜː/
f**or**ty	b**ur**ger

Spelling: silent letters (2)

3 **S** We don't say every letter in some words. Write the silent letters.

1 wa _l_ k
2 g __ itar
3 __ rong
4 fr __ ends
5 int __ resting
6 diff __ rent
7 y __ ung

8 g __ ide book
9 __ rote
10 sc __ ool
11 cent __ e
12 pe __ ple
13 gran __ father
14 dau __ ter

Reading and Writing Portfolio 9 p68

10A Life changes

Language Summary 10, Student's Book p132

Future plans VOCABULARY 10.1

1 Fill in the gaps with these words.

| ~~school~~ | house | engaged | new | exam |
| course | city | flat | university | |

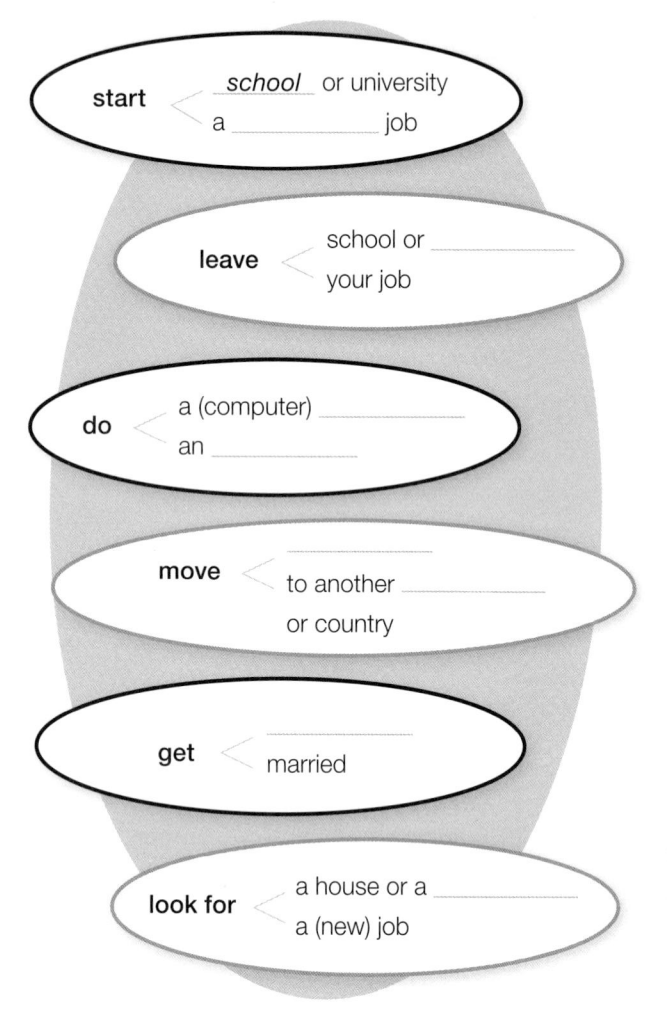

- start — _school_ or university / a _____ job
- leave — school or _____ / your job
- do — a (computer) _____ / an _____
- move — _____ to another _____ or country
- get — _____ married
- look for — a house or a _____ / a (new) job

Future time phrases VOCABULARY 10.2

2 Put these future time phrases in order.

a tonight *1*
b next year
c tomorrow evening
d in 2030
e in December
f tomorrow night
g next Tuesday
h tomorrow afternoon

be going to: positive and negative GRAMMAR 10.1

3 Read about these people's plans. Fill in the gaps with the correct form of *be going to* and the verbs in brackets ( ). Use contractions (*I'm*, *she's*, *aren't*, etc.) if possible.

I ¹ _'m going to leave_ (leave) university in July, but I ² _____ _____ (not look for) a job. In August my brother and I ³ _____ (travel) around Europe together. We ⁴ _____ (not drive), we ⁵ _____ (go) by train.

Meg and I ⁶ _____ (move) to Paris next month. I ⁷ _____ (start) a new job at a TV company. Meg ⁸ _____ (not look for) a job, she ⁹ _____ (write) a book about life in France.

Toby and I ¹⁰ _____ (get) married in September, but we ¹¹ _____ (not have) a big wedding, only about 20 or 30 people. And for our honeymoon* we ¹² _____ (go) to Mexico – that's where we met five years ago!

*a honeymoon = the holiday after your wedding

Review: negatives (2)

4 Make these sentences negative.

1 I'm going to look for a new job.
   I'm not going to look for a new job.
2 I like shopping for clothes.
3 My parents are going to move house.
4 I went out with friends last night.
5 Katherine works at home.
6 There's a station near my flat.
7 I can play the piano.
8 Lisa and Zak have a dog.

Review: question words and Past Simple *Wh-* questions

5 a Fill in the gaps with *did*, *was* or *were*.

1 How old _were_ you in this photo?
2 Where _____ you born?
3 How much _____ you spend yesterday?
4 What _____ your grandfather's job?
5 How many shirts _____ you buy?
6 When _____ your mother born?
7 Why _____ you late for class?
8 Who _____ you go on holiday with?

b Match answers a–h to questions 1–8.

a Because the train was late. ___
b He was a doctor. ___
c About £30. ___
d I was 16. *1*
e I was born in Moscow. ___
f My friend Jennifer. ___
g In 1960. ___
h Three. ___

10B A new start

Phrases with *have*, *watch*, *go*, *go to* VOCABULARY 10.3

1 S Write the words.

1 w _a t c h_ TV
2 h _____ d _____ with f _____ s
3 g__ r_____
4 w_____ the n____
5 g__ s_____
6 g__ to the c_____
7 g__ to the g___
8 g__ s_____
9 w_____ s_____ on __
10 h_____ c_____ with f_____
11 h____ a p____
12 g__ to a p____

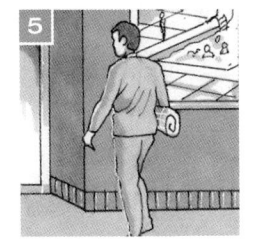

49

be going to: questions and short answers

GRAMMAR 10.2

2 Read the conversations. Fill in the gaps in questions 1–7.

LUCY ¹What _are_ you _going_ to _do_ next weekend?
GINA Dave and I are going to fly to Paris for the weekend.
LUCY ²Where _____ you _____ to stay?
GINA With an old friend from university. She has a big flat near the airport. And what about you? ³What _____ you _____ _____ do next weekend?
LUCY Well, I'm going to go shopping on Saturday.
GINA ⁴What _____ _____ _____ _____ buy?
LUCY A new camera – and some new shoes!

ALEX ⁵_____ are _____ going _____ do after the course?
HUGO I'm going to look for a job.
ALEX And what about Laura? ⁶_____ she _____ _____ do?
HUGO She's going to do a teaching course.
ALEX Really? ⁷_____ _____ _____ _____ study?
HUGO In Cambridge.

3 a Make questions with these words.

1 going to / Are / fly / Gina and Dave / to Paris ?
   Are Gina and Dave going to fly to Paris?
2 in a hotel / going to / they / Are / stay ?
   _____
3 going to / on Saturday / Lucy / shopping / Is / go ?
   _____
4 she / going to / Is / a new laptop / buy ?
   _____
5 look for / Is / a job / Hugo / going to ?
   _____
6 Laura / going to / Is / a German course / do ?
   _____

b Read the conversations in **2** again. Then write short answers for the questions in **3a**.

1 _Yes, they are._
2 _____
3 _____
4 _____
5 _____
6 _____

Review: short answers

4 a Match questions 1–8 to short answers a–h.

1 Are you a student?   a Yes, he is.
2 Is he married?   b Yes, there is.
3 Do you like tennis?   c Yes, I am.
4 Does he have a car?   d Yes, there are.
5 Can you swim?   e Yes, I do.
6 Is there a bank?   f Yes, I did.
7 Are there any shops?   g Yes, he does.
8 Did you see her?   h Yes, I can.

b Write the negative short answers for the questions in **4a**.

1 _No, I'm not._
2 _____
3 _____
4 _____
5 _____
6 _____
7 _____
8 _____

10C ▶ REAL WORLD — Good luck!

Adjectives (3): feelings VOCABULARY 10.4

1 S Write the adjectives.

1 s _a_ d
2 e _ _ _ _ _ _ _ d
3 h _ _ _ _ _ y
4 s _ _ _ _ _ _ d
5 t _ _ _ _ d  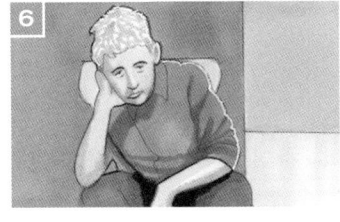  
6 b _ _ _ _ d
7 h _ _ _ _ _ _ y
8 a _ _ _ _ y

Saying goodbye and good luck REAL WORLD 10.1

2 Fill in the gaps with these phrases.

> Have a good
> a lot
> Yes, see you
> See you in

BOB Right, it's time to go.
SUE Bye, Bob. ¹ _Have a good_ holiday.
BOB Thanks ² _____ .
SUE ³ _____ three weeks.
BOB ⁴ _____ . Bye.

> good luck with
> Have a good
> See you
> very much

TED Are you here next week?
LIZ No, I'm going to China on Monday.
TED ⁵ _____ time.
LIZ Thanks. And ⁶ _____ your new job.
TED Thank you ⁷ _____ .
LIZ ⁸ _____ next month.
TED Yes, see you. Bye.

Pronunciation: syllables and word stress (2)

3 Write these words in the table.

> happy   difficult   fantastic   nineteenth
> animals   boring   guitar   amazing   April
> basketball   July   December

•dancing	••fourteenth
happy	
•••yesterday	••September

Spelling: Past Simple verb forms

4 S Write the Past Simple of these irregular verbs.

1 tell   _t o l d_   6 write   _____
2 give   _____   7 go   _____
3 come _____   8 leave   _____
4 buy   _____   9 have   _____
5 meet   _____   10 get   _____

▶ Reading and Writing Portfolio 10 p70

Reading and Writing Portfolio 1

Where are you from?

Reading three conversations
Writing full stops (.) and question marks (?); capital letters (1); about you
Review *I, my, you, your*; *he, his, she, her*; countries; the alphabet

Felix *Brigitte*

1 Look at the photo. Put this conversation in order.

FELIX
  a Nice to meet you.
  b Hello, I'm Felix Hofmann. *1*
  c I'm from Germany. And you?

BRIGITTE
  d You too. Where are you from?
  e I'm from Paris.
  f Hello, my name's Brigitte Laurent. *2*

HELP WITH WRITING
Full stops (.) and question marks (?)

2 Read about full stops and question marks.
  • We use a full stop (.) at the end of a sentence.
    Hello, I'm Felix Hofmann.
  • We use a question mark (?) at the end of a question.
    Where are you from?

3 a Make sentences or questions with these words. Write the full stops and question marks.

  1 name / your / What's
     What's your name?

  2 from / Where / you / are

  3 William / name's / My

  4 from / Where's / she

  5 the UK / from / I'm

  6 you / are / How

  7 the USA / from / She's

  8 thanks / fine, / I'm

b Match the questions and answers in **3a**.

question	answer
1	3

HELP WITH WRITING Capital letters (1)

4 In English we use capital letters (A, B, C, etc.) for these things.
  • At the beginning of a sentence: **N**ice to meet you.
  • For *I*: Hello, **I**'m Felix Hofmann.
  • For countries: *I'm from **G**ermany.*
  • For cities: *I'm from **P**aris.*
  • For names: *Hello, my name's **B**rigitte **L**aurent.*

TIPS • We use capital letters for *the* **UK** and *the* **USA**.
  • We don't use capital letters with things: *It's a camera.* not *It's a ~~C~~amera.*

5 Write these sentences with capital letters.

1 his name's robin jones.
   His name's Robin Jones.

2 luciano's from italy.

3 where's elizabeth from?

4 alexei's from moscow.

5 hello, i'm david smith.

6 nick's from bristol, in the uk.

7 she's from orlando, in the usa.

6 Write the conversations. Use capital letters, full stops and question marks.

1

A what's your first name
   What's your first name?

B it's abdul

A what's your surname

B it's razzaq

2

A where are you from

B i'm from brazil and you

A i'm from izmir, in turkey

B nice to meet you

A you too

7 a Fill in the table for you.

1	first name	
2	surname	
3	country	
4	mobile number	
5	home number	

b Write five sentences about you. Use the information in **7a**. Use capital letters and full stops.

1 My first name's
2
3
4
5

Tick (✓) the things you can do in English in the Reading and Writing Progress Portfolio, p72.

Reading and Writing Portfolio 2

Three people

Reading business cards; addresses; forms
Writing capital letters (2); filling in a form
Review be (singular); jobs; personal information questions

1 Look at the photos. Match people 1–3 to business cards A–C.

A  Scott Davis
Musician
26 Kent Street
Sydney NSW 2000
Australia
☏ 02 9321 4577
email: s.davis@gmail.net

B City Computers
196 Cedar Street
Seattle WA 98121
USA
Janet Richards
Manager
☎ 206 818 7904
email: j.richards@cc.com

C Lucy Smith
Actress
76 Queen Street
Manchester M18 3JS
UK
home: 0161 284 9865
mobile: 07986 342187
email: lucy.smith@webmail.co.uk

2 Read the business cards again. Choose the correct answers.

1. Scott Davis is *a manager* / *a musician*.
2. He's from *Seattle* / *Sydney*.
3. His email address is *s.davis@gmail.net* / *sdavis@gmailnet*.
4. Janet Richards is *British* / *American*.
5. She's *a manager* / *a musician*.
6. Her phone number is *206 181 7904* / *206 818 7904*.
7. Lucy Smith is *a musician* / *an actress*.
8. She's *British* / *American*.
9. Her *home* / *mobile* number is 07986 342187.

HELP WITH WRITING Capital letters (2)

3 a When do we use capital letters (A, B, C, etc.) in English? Check in **4** on p52.

b We also use capital letters for these things.
- titles: **M**r, **M**rs, **M**s, **M**iss
- addresses: 76 **Q**ueen **S**treet, **M**anchester
- postcodes: **M**18 3**JS**
- companies: **C**ity **C**omputers
- nationalities: She's **A**merican.

TIP • *postcode* (UK) = *zip code* (US)

5 Look at Lucy's business card again. Complete the online hotel form.

PH
PARK HOTEL

Registration form

first name _Lucy_
surname _____
nationality _British_
address _____
_____
postcode _____
home number _____
mobile number _____
email address _____
room number _617_

6 Fill in the form for you.

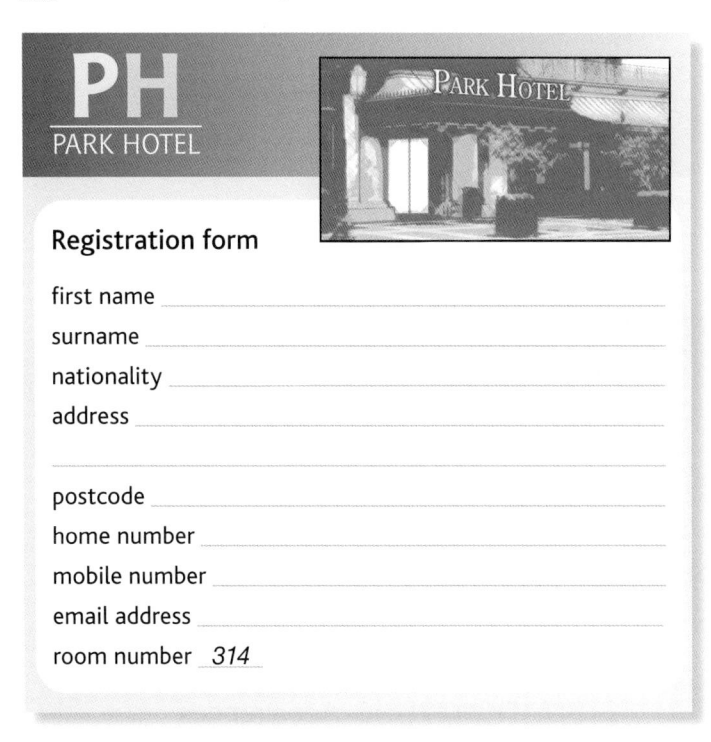

PH
PARK HOTEL

Registration form

first name _____
surname _____
nationality _____
address _____
_____
postcode _____
home number _____
mobile number _____
email address _____
room number _314_

Tick (✓) the things you can do in English in the Reading and Writing Progress Portfolio, p72.

4 a Look at the business cards again. (Circle) all the capital letters.

b Write these sentences with capital letters.

1 scott davis is american.
   Scott Davis is American.

2 is benetton an italian company?
   _____

3 her name is mrs alice roberts.
   _____

4 are you mr henry long?
   _____

5 ford is an american company.
   _____

6 her address is 1306 south beach, miami.
   _____

7 my address is 26 new street, london sw19 4gp.
   _____

Reading and Writing Portfolio 3

See you soon!

Reading holiday emails
Writing apostrophes; *and* and *but*; a holiday email
Review adjectives; *be*; short answers

1 a Check these words in a dictionary.

| on holiday   a beach   a bridge   amazing |

b Read the email. Then choose the correct short answers.

To: daniela.robertson@webmail.net

Hi Daniela
How are you? We're on holiday in San Francisco, in the USA! We're in a small hotel near the beach. Our room is nice, but it isn't very big. Brian's brother is in the USA too, but he isn't in San Francisco, he's in Los Angeles. The people here are very friendly and we love the restaurants and cafés. The food is good and it's very cheap. Oh, and the Golden Gate Bridge is amazing!
See you soon!
Love Jane and Brian

The Golden Gate Bridge, San Francisco

1 Are Jane and Brian in San Francisco?
 (a) Yes, they are. b No, they aren't.
2 Are they in a big hotel?
 a Yes, they are. b No, they aren't.
3 Is their hotel near the beach?
 a Yes, it is. b No, it isn't.
4 Is their room very big?
 a Yes, it is. b No, it isn't.
5 Is Brian's brother in San Francisco?
 a Yes, he is. b No, he isn't.
6 Are the people very friendly?
 a Yes, they are. b No, they aren't.
7 Is the food very expensive?
 a Yes, it is. b No, it isn't.

HELP WITH WRITING Apostrophes

2 We use apostrophes (') for these things.
- Contractions with *be* (*I'm*, *you're*, *isn't*, etc.): **We're** *in a small hotel.*
- Possessive *'s*: **Brian's** *brother*

3 Write these sentences again with apostrophes.

1 Toms father isnt a doctor.
 Tom's father isn't a doctor.
2 Im an actor and shes a teacher.
 _____
3 Youre Sallys brother.
 _____
4 They arent Bobs children.
 _____
5 Were in Mr Wests English class.
 _____
6 Theyre French and hes Italian.
 _____
7 Whats your fathers name?
 _____
8 Wheres Jacks wife from?
 _____
9 Marys mother isnt from the UK.
 _____
10 Whos Helenas English teacher?
 _____

HELP WITH WRITING *and* and *but*

4 a Look at these sentences. Notice how we use *and* and *but*.

positive (+)   **positive (+)**
The food is good.   It's very cheap.
The food is good **and** it's very cheap.

positive (+)   **negative (–)**
Our room is nice.   It isn't very big.
Our room is nice, **but** it isn't very big.

TIP • We sometimes use a comma (,) before *but*.

b Look again at Jane and Brian's email in **1b**. Underline *and* and *but*.

5 Write these sentences again with *and* or *but*.

1 Our room is nice. It's very big.
   Our room is nice and it's very big.

2 Our hotel is very cheap. It isn't near the beach.

3 The restaurant is nice. The food is very good.

4 I love fruit. I eat a lot of vegetables.

5 She's a German teacher. She isn't from Germany.

6 They're my friends. They aren't in my class.

7 Simon's my son. Yvonne's my daughter.

8 Brian is friendly. His brother is very unfriendly.

9 She's from London. She's an actress.

6 Read this email. Fill in the gaps with *and* or *but*.

To: greg.wilson100@netmail.org

Hi Greg
How are you? I'm on holiday in Rome! I'm in a small hotel near the Colosseum. My room is nice ¹_____ it's very cheap. My sister Angie is in Rome too, ²_____ my brother isn't here. The people are very friendly, ³_____ my Italian isn't very good! The food is very nice ⁴_____ I love the pasta here.
See you soon!
Best wishes Evelyn

The Colosseum, Rome

7 Imagine you are on holiday. Write an email to a friend. Use these phrases.

Hi (name)
How are you? I'm on holiday in … !
I'm in a … hotel near … .
My room is … and / but … .
(name) is in … too.
The people are … and / but … .
The food is … and / but … .
See you soon!
Love / Best wishes

Tick (✓) the things you can do in English in the Reading and Writing Progress Portfolio, p72.

Reading and Writing Portfolio 4

Internet profiles

Reading two internet profiles
Writing word order (1) and (2); an internet profile
Review phrases with *like*, *have*, *live*, *work*, *study*; free time activities; Present Simple (*I*, *you*, *we*, *th*

www.mybook.net/dannygreen/profile

Mybook Chat to your friends around the world!

username:
password:
sign in

home | profile | friends | messages | search:

HOME
I live in a big flat in Notting Hill with three friends.

WORK
I work for a TV company in the centre of London.

FAMILY
I have two brothers, Sam and Pat, and a sister, Rachel.

FREE TIME
I watch TV and I play video games.
I study Spanish at a language school.
I go to the cinema a lot.
I go to concerts with my friends.
I love Chinese and Mexican food.

NAME Danny Green
NATIONALITY British
MARRIED / SINGLE single
TOWN / CITY London
COUNTRY UK

Click <u>here</u> to be Danny's friend.

---

1 Read Danny's internet profile. Tick (✓) the true sentences. Change one word in the false sentences.

1 Danny's surname is Green. ✓
2 He's ~~American~~.
   British
3 He's married.
4 His flat is in Notting Hill, in London.
5 Three people live in his flat.
6 Sam and Pat are Danny's sisters.
7 Danny and his friends go to concerts.

HELP WITH WRITING Word order (1)

2 a Look at these sentences. Notice the word order and the verbs in bold.

I **have** two brothers.
I **play** video games.
I **study** Spanish.

b Look at these sentences. Notice the word order and the prepositions (*in*, etc.).

I **live** <u>in</u> a big flat.
I **work** <u>for</u> a TV company.
I **go** <u>to</u> the cinema a lot.

TIP • Adjectives go before nouns:
a **big** flat not ~~a flat big~~.

www.mybook.net/sarahnewman/profile

HOME
I ¹ _live in_ a nice house in ² _____ Edinburgh with my husband, Brian, and our two children.

WORK
I work in a ³ _____ three days a week.

FAMILY
Brian and I ⁴ _____, Freddie, and a daughter, Vicky.

FREE TIME
I play ⁵ _____ a lot.
I go ⁶ _____ with my friends.
I study Chinese at ⁷ _____.
I watch DVDs with ⁸ _____.

Click here to be Sarah's friend.

NAME Sarah Newman
NATIONALITY American
MARRIED / SINGLE married
TOWN / CITY Edinburgh
COUNTRY UK

---

3 Make sentences with these words.

1 have / Barbara and I / children / two .
   Barbara and I have two children.
2 big / work / I / office / a / in / very .
   _____
3 a / have / My / car / new / grandparents .
   _____
4 go / concerts / don't / to / My wife and I .
   _____
5 very / live / in / I / small / flat / a .
   _____
6 languages / Our / London / study / in / children .
   _____

HELP WITH WRITING Word order (2)

4 a We usually put extra information (people, places, etc.) at the end of the sentence. Look at these examples in bold.

1 I live in a big flat **in Notting Hill with three friends**.
2 I work for a TV company **in the centre of London**.
3 I study Spanish **at a language school**.

b Underline the prepositions in the sentences in **4a**.

TIP • We put **a lot** at the end of the sentence:
I go to the cinema **a lot**.

5 Read Sarah's internet profile. Fill in the gaps with these words and phrases.

> ~~live in~~   have a son   the centre of
> tennis   to the cinema   hotel
> a language school   my children

6 a Write notes in the table for you.

HOME	
WORK	
FAMILY	
FREE TIME	

b Write your internet profile. Use your notes in **6a**. Check your word order.

Tick (✓) the things you can do in English in the Reading and Writing Progress Portfolio, p72.

Reading and Writing Portfolio 5

My best friend

Reading best friends
Writing *because* and *also*; my best friend
Review *and* and *but*; Present Simple; free time activities; frequency adverbs and phrases with *every*

1 a Check these words in a dictionary.

> a best friend   Ireland   Scotland
> a journalist   a vegetarian

b Read about Juliet's best friend, Katie. Choose the correct words in these sentences.

1. Katie lives in (Ireland) / *the UK*.
2. She *is* / *isn't* married.
3. She's a *music* / *sports* journalist.
4. She's *a musician* / *a singer* in a rock band.
5. She goes *shopping* / *to the cinema* in her free time.
6. She *eats* / *doesn't eat* chicken.
7. She *sometimes* / *never* has Italian food.
8. She *likes* / *doesn't like* coffee.
9. Juliet *lives* / *doesn't live* in Dublin.
10. Juliet *always* / *never* sees Katie on her birthday.

My best friend's name is Katie. She lives in Dublin, in Ireland. She's 29 and she's single. Katie's always very busy because she has two jobs. She's a music journalist for a newspaper in Dublin. She's also a singer in a rock band.

In her free time she goes to the cinema. She also eats out a lot. She doesn't eat meat because she's a vegetarian. She loves Chinese and Italian food. She also drinks six espressos a day!

I don't see Katie very much because I live in London, but we're always together on our birthdays because they're on the same day!

HELP WITH WRITING *because* and *also*

BECAUSE

2 a Look at these sentences. Notice when we use *because*.

Katie's always very busy **because** she has two jobs.
She doesn't eat meat **because** she's a vegetarian.

ALSO

b Look at these sentences. Notice when we use *also*.

She's a music journalist for a newspaper in Dublin. She's **also** a singer in a rock band.
In her free time she goes to the cinema. She **also** eats out a lot.

c We use *also* in positive (+) sentences. Read these rules and the examples.

- *Also* goes after *be*:
  She**'s also** a singer in a rock band.
- *Also* goes before other verbs:
  She **also eats** out a lot.

3 a Look again at the text about Katie. Underline all the examples of *because* and *also*.

b Circle all the examples of *and* and *but* in the text about Katie.

Katie   Juliet

4 Fill in the gaps with *and*, *but* or *because*.

1 I speak Russian _because_ my mother's from Moscow.
2 I get up at 7.00 _____ I have breakfast at 7.30.
3 He never eats fish _____ he doesn't like it.
4 She loves music, _____ she never goes to concerts.
5 I like Francesca _____ she's very friendly.
6 They speak Italian, _____ they don't speak Spanish.
7 I always drink black coffee _____ I don't like milk.
8 In my free time I watch TV _____ I play video games.

5 Put *also* in the correct place in the sentences in bold.

                   also
1 He plays football. **He ∧ plays tennis.**
2 That car is beautiful. **It's very expensive.**
3 She has three cats. **She has a dog.**
4 Kevin's an actor. **He's a musician.**
5 Gina loves lasagne. **She likes pizza.**

6 Read about Clive's best friend, Steve. Choose the correct words.

My best friend's name is Steve. He's 34 ¹(and) / *but* he lives in Glasgow, in Scotland. He's married ²*and* / *but* he has two children. He's a teacher ³*and* / *because* he ⁴*and* / *also* writes children's books. He's always tired ⁵*because* / *but* he works six days a week. In his free time he watches DVDs ⁶*and* / *but* he loves going to the cinema. He likes Italian and Mexican food, ⁷*and* / *but* he doesn't like Japanese food. He ⁸*also* / *because* loves ice cream. I see Steve every weekend ⁹*because* / *also* we play football together. I ¹⁰*also* / *and* see him after work in the week.

7 a Make notes about your best friend.

name	
age	
lives in	
married / single	
children	
job	
free time	
likes / doesn't like	
when I see him / her	

b Write about your best friend. Use *because*, *also* and your notes in **7a**.

Tick (✓) the things you can do in English in the Reading and Writing Progress Portfolio, p72.

Reading and Writing Portfolio 6

A tourist in London

Reading a newspaper article
Writing describing places; places for tourists in your town or city
Review *there is / there are*; places in a town or city; *and*, *but*, *also*

1 a Check these words in a dictionary.

visit   high
summer   an adult
a tube station   free
popular   young

b Read about the London Eye, the British Museum and Covent Garden. Answer these questions.

1 Is there a shop at the London Eye?
   Yes, there is.

2 How much is the London Eye for two adults and a three-year-old child?

3 What tube station do you go to for the London Eye?

4 Are there any cafés at the British Museum?

5 Is the British Museum open on Mondays?

6 Is the British Museum open in the evening?

7 Is Covent Garden in the centre of London?

8 Are there any places to eat in Covent Garden?

9 Are there any theatres near Covent Garden?

LONDON'S TOP FIVE PLACES

There are hundreds of things to see and do in London. Here are our top five places for tourists to visit.

❶ The London Eye

The London Eye is a great place to visit. You can see a lot of London's famous buildings from the top because it's 135m high! There's also a shop and two good cafés. In the summer the London Eye is open from 10.00 a.m. to 9.30 p.m. every day. Adults (16+) £18.90, Children (4–15) £11.10, Children (0–4) free.

🚇 Waterloo

❷ The British Museum

The British Museum is the best museum in London. There are a lot of interesting things to see and the building is also very beautiful. There are some nice cafés, a very good restaurant and a bookshop. The museum is open from 10.00 a.m. to 5.30 p.m. every day – and it's free!

🚇 Tottenham Court Road

❸ Covent Garden

Covent Garden is a big market in the centre of the city. It's a great place to go shopping and it's very popular with tourists. You can also see some of the best street entertainers* in London. There are a lot of nice places to eat in Covent Garden and it's also near London's theatres and cinemas.

🚇 Covent Garden

🚇 = tube station   *street entertainers = people who play music, sing, etc. in the street for money

HELP WITH WRITING Describing places

2 **a** Read about the London Eye, the British Museum and Covent Garden again. (Circle) *There's* and *There are*.

(There are) hundreds of things to see and do in London.

b Underline these phrases in the article. Check you understand them.

… is a great place to (visit).
You can (also) …
… is open from (10.00 a.m.) to (9.30 p.m.) every day.
… is the best (museum) in (London).
… is very popular with (tourists).

4 Camden Market

Camden Market ¹ *is the best* market in London and it's ² _____ young people. It's ³ _____ buy clothes and ⁴ _____ buy food and things for the home. ⁵ _____ also some nice cafés. The market ⁶ _____ 10 a.m. to 6 p.m. every day, but the weekend is the best time to visit.

Ⓣ Camden Town

5 Hyde Park

Hyde Park is ⁷ _____ tourists. ⁸ _____ play football or tennis there, and it's ⁹ _____ have a picnic*.
¹⁰ _____ a very nice restaurant in the park and ¹¹ _____ sometimes concerts at the weekend. The park is open from 5 a.m. to midnight ¹² _____ .

Ⓣ Hyde Park Corner

3 Read about Camden Market and Hyde Park. Fill in the gaps with these phrases.

CAMDEN MARKET

<s>is the best</s>	you can also
very popular with	is open from
There are	a great place to

HYDE PARK

There's also	there are
a great place to	every day
very popular with	You can

4 Read about Camden Market and Hyde Park again. Are these sentences true (T) or false (F)?

1 Young people like Camden Market. *T*
2 You can buy clothes and food there.
3 The market is closed on Sundays.
4 You can't play tennis in Hyde Park.
5 You can have lunch in the park.
6 Hyde Park opens early in the morning.

5 **a** Write the names of three places for tourists to visit in your town or city.

1 _____
2 _____
3 _____

b Write about the places in **5a**. Use *There's*, *There are* and phrases from **2b**.

Tick (✓) the things you can do in English in the Reading and Writing Progress Portfolio, p72.

have a picnic = eat your food in a park

63

Reading and Writing Portfolio 7

The same or different?

Reading people in my family
Writing sentences with *and*, *but* and object pronouns; word order (3): *both* and *together*
Review *love*, *like*, *hate*; frequency adverbs and phrases with *every*

1 a Check you know these words.

| the same | different | both | together |

b Read about Charlie and Rob. Are these sentences true (T) or false (F)?

1 Charlie and Rob are brothers. **T**
2 They like the same music.
3 They both like watching DVDs.
4 They don't like tennis.
5 Rob likes getting up early.
6 Charlie doesn't like cats.
7 Rob doesn't like shopping for clothes.
8 Charlie eats burgers and chips every day.

HELP WITH WRITING
Sentences with *and*, *but* and object pronouns

2 We don't usually repeat words in sentences with *and* and *but*. Look at these examples. Notice the object pronouns (*it*, *them*, etc.).

I love (shopping for clothes), but Rob hates (it).

Rob doesn't like (cats), but I love (them).

(Rob) is the best brother in the world and I love (him) very much.

My brother's name is Rob and we both like a lot of the same things. We both like the same bands and we usually go to concerts together. We're both very busy in the week, but I go to Rob's flat at the weekend and we watch DVDs together. We also play tennis every Sunday morning, but Rob's always late because he hates getting up early!

Rob and I are also very different. He doesn't like cats, but I love them. And I love shopping for clothes, but Rob hates it. He usually wears a T-shirt, jeans and trainers! And we don't like the same food. I usually eat vegetables and fruit, and he eats burgers and chips every day! I think Rob is the best brother in the world and I love him very much.

3 Write sentences with *and* and *but*. Change the words in **bold** to object pronouns.

1 I love tennis. My sister hates **tennis**.
I love tennis, but my sister hates it.

2 Tom doesn't like dogs. I love **dogs**.
_____

3 Anna's my best friend. I email **Anna** every day.
_____

4 I love rock music. My sister doesn't like **rock music**.
_____

5 Pete's my son. I love **Pete** very much.
_____

6 I love horror films. My wife hates **horror films**.
_____

Charlie   Rob

HELP WITH WRITING
Word order (3): *both* and *together*

4 Read these rules and the examples.
- *Both* goes after *be*:
  We**'re both** very busy in the week.
- *Both* goes before other verbs:
  We **both like** the same bands.
- *Together* is usually at the end of the sentence: We watch DVDs **together**.

TIPS • Frequency adverbs (*always*, etc.) go after *be* and before other verbs:
Rob**'s always** late.
We **usually go** to concerts together.

• Phrases with *every* are usually at the end of the sentence:
He eats burgers and chips **every day**.

5 Read about Charlie and Rob again. Underline all the examples of *both*, *together*, frequency adverbs and phrases with *every*. Notice the word order.

6 Read about Daisy and Lisa. Put the words in brackets ( ) in the correct place in the sentences.

(**both** →) My daughter's name is Daisy and
             both
we ⋏ like a lot of the same things. (**both, together** →) We love clothes and sometimes go shopping. (**both** →) And we love black and white films. (**usually, together** →) On Sunday afternoons we watch an old film. With a big box of chocolates, of course!

Daisy and I are also very different. (**it** →) She doesn't like flying, but I love. (**them** →) And I like soap operas, but Daisy hates. (**every evening** →) I watch two soap operas. (**it** →) Daisy also loves cooking, but I hate. (**every day** →) In our home my husband cooks dinner! (**her** →) I think Daisy is the best daughter in the world and I love very much.

7 Read about Daisy and Lisa again. Find three things they both love.

8 Write a profile of you and a person in your family. Use these phrases and your own ideas.

> My …'s name is … and we both like a lot of the same things.
> We both like / love …
> We always / usually / sometimes … together.
> … and I are also very different.
> … doesn't like … , but I love it / them.
> And I like / love … , but … hates it / them.
> I think … is the best … in the world and I love him / her very much.

Tick (✓) the things you can do in English in the Reading and Writing Progress Portfolio, p72.

Daisy   Lisa

Reading and Writing Portfolio 8

Going out

Reading entertainment adverts; emails
Writing a / an and the; your last film, play or rock concert
Review Past Simple of be; adjectives; time phrases with on, in, at

1 a Look at these adverts for things to do in Birmingham, a city in the UK. Match adverts 1–4 to a–d.

- a a play _____
- b a classical concert _____
- c a film _____
- d a rock concert _____

b Read the adverts again. Answer these questions.

1 When is the Big Noise concert?
   It's on Saturday 24th March.
2 What number do you phone to buy tickets for this concert?
   _____
3 Where can you see *Victoria's Wedding*?
   _____
4 Where can you buy tickets online for this play?
   _____
5 Where can you see the film *The Phone Call*?
   _____
6 Who is the actress in this film?
   _____
7 What time does the classical concert start?
   _____
8 How much are the tickets for this concert?
   _____

---

1 Harry Lee   Julia Ross

THE PHONE CALL

15

***** 'The best film of the year'
Joe Green, THE DAILY NEWS

OPENS FRIDAY 23rd MARCH
The Apollo Cinema, Birmingham
0870 947 4331
Book online at
www.theapollo.co.uk

---

2 Michael SIMONS   Catherine FULLER

in

Victoria's Wedding

FRIDAY 23rd MARCH TO
THURSDAY 19th APRIL

THE CITY THEATRE
New Street,
Birmingham B5 3YP

0845 345 9776
or online at
www.thecitytheatre.co.uk

'A great evening out
for all the family'
Birmingham Express

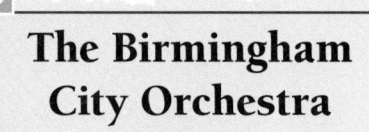

3

The Birmingham City Orchestra

PRESENTS

An evening of Mozart,
Beethoven and Brahms

Fairwell Hall, Market Street,
Birmingham B3 5TG

Saturday 24th March at 7.30 p.m.

Tickets £30, £25 and £20
Credit cards 0845 234 7866

Book online at
www.fairwellhall.co.uk

4

Big Noise

Saturday 24th March Birmingham Arena
Credit cards Tel 0844 782 1176 Buy online at www.yourtickets.com

New album 'Never Say Never' out April 13th
www.bignoiserock.com

2 Read email A. Where was Mia last Saturday?

A

Hi Judy

How are you? Paul and I went* to a concert last Saturday. Do you know Big Noise? They're a rock band from London. The concert was fantastic! It was at the Birmingham Arena in the city centre and there were about 3,000 people there. The band played* for two hours and the singer was amazing. Big Noise are now my favourite band! How was your weekend?
Love Mia

*went = Past Simple of go
*played = Past Simple of play

HELP WITH WRITING a / an and the

3 Read these rules and the examples.
- We use *a* or *an* to talk about one of many places, people or things: They're **a rock band** from London. (There are a lot of rock bands from London.)
- We use *the* when there is only one place, person or thing: It was at **the Birmingham Arena**. (There's only one place with this name.)
- We use *a / an* to talk about a person, place or thing for the first time: Paul and I went to (**a concert**) last Saturday.
- We use *the* to talk about the person, place or thing again: (**The concert**) was fantastic!

TIP • We also use *the* in these phrases:
in **the** city centre
go to **the** cinema / theatre
in **the** morning / afternoon / evening
at **the** weekend

4 Read email B. Fill in the gaps with *a* or *the*.

B

Hi Mia

I'm pleased that ¹ _the_ concert was good. My weekend was OK. On Saturday I had* lunch with ² _____ friend in ³ _____ café. Then in ⁴ _____ evening I went to ⁵ _____ cinema with Gary. We went to see ⁶ _____ film, but it wasn't very good. ⁷ _____ film was called 'The Phone Call' and it was very long and boring. After ⁸ _____ film we went to ⁹ _____ pizza restaurant in ¹⁰ _____ city centre. ¹¹ _____ restaurant wasn't very full, but ¹² _____ pizzas were fantastic! Have a good day!
Lots of love Judy

*had = Past Simple of have

5 Write about the last film, play or rock concert you went to. Use these phrases and your own ideas.

I went to a *film / play / concert* … (when?). It was at the … in … (where?). The *film / play / band* was called … (what?). I went with … (who?) and there were … (how many?) people there. The … was *fantastic / OK / boring*. After the *film / play / concert* we went … (where?). We had a … (what?) and … . It was a *great / fantastic / terrible* evening.

Tick (✓) the things you can do in English in the Reading and Writing Progress Portfolio, p72.

Reading and Writing Portfolio 9

On holiday

Reading a travel blog; a holiday in France
Writing *because*, *so*, *when*; your last holiday
Review Past Simple; transport; holiday activities; *and* and *but*

WRITE A TRAVEL BLOG

HOME | FORUM | BLOGS | TRAVEL GUIDE | TICKETS | SEARCH

Ollie and Jo in Mexico

Tuesday 25th July

Jo and I arrived in Mexico City at 7 a.m. on Sunday. We were very tired because we didn't sleep on the plane. When we arrived at our hotel, we slept for nine hours. Yesterday we went sightseeing in the centre. There are lots of beautiful buildings and some interesting markets. And we're both very happy because we're on holiday!

Thursday 27th July

Yesterday we went to Teotihuacan, an ancient city about 45 minutes away. It was amazing! We walked around the Pyramid of the Sun and Jo took some great photos. When we got back to Mexico City, we had dinner near the hotel. Jo can speak Spanish so she ordered the food. My Spanish is terrible!

Sunday 30th July

Hi again – we're in Cancún! We arrived two days ago and it's very hot here – about 38°C. The beaches in Cancún are very busy so yesterday we went to Isla Holbox, a small island about 16 km away. We loved Isla Holbox because it was very quiet. We watched the sunset and had dinner on the beach – the fish was fantastic!

1
a Check these words in a dictionary.

> ancient   a pyramid   quiet   a sunset

b Read the blog about Ollie and Jo's holiday in Mexico. Put photos A–C in order.

c Read about Ollie and Jo's holiday again. Choose the correct words.

1. Ollie and Jo arrived in Mexico in the *morning* / *evening*.
2. On Monday they *slept a lot* / *went sightseeing*.
3. Teotihuacan is *in* / *near* Mexico City.
4. *Ollie* / *Jo* can't speak Spanish.
5. They arrived in Cancún on *Friday* / *Saturday*.
6. They had fish for dinner in *Cancún* / *Isla Holbox*.

68

HELP WITH WRITING *because*, *so* and *when*

BECAUSE AND SO

2 a Look at these sentences. Notice the difference between *because* and *so*.

1 a We were very tired **because** we didn't sleep on the plane.
  b We didn't sleep on the plane **so** we were very tired.
2 a Jo can speak Spanish **so** she ordered the food.
  b Jo ordered the food **because** she can speak Spanish.

TIP • We usually put *because* and *so* in the middle of the sentence.

WHEN

b Look at this sentence. Notice how we use *when*.

　　　first　　　　　　second
When we arrived at our hotel, we slept for nine hours.

TIPS • We can put *when* at the beginning or in the middle of the sentence:
We slept for nine hours **when** we got to our hotel.
• We usually use a comma (,) if *when* is at the beginning of the sentence:
When we got to our hotel, we slept for nine hours.

3 Read about Ollie and Jo's holiday again. Underline all the examples of *because*, *so* and *when*.

4 Write these sentences with *because*, *so* or *when*. There is sometimes more than one answer.

1 I didn't go swimming. I can't swim.
　I didn't go swimming because I can't swim.
2 I was very tired. I went to bed early.

3 We arrived in Paris. We went for a walk.

4 He went by train. He hates flying.

5 I got home. I phoned my sister.

6 There weren't any taxis. We rented a car.

5 a Read about Kathy's last holiday. Where did she go? Did she have a good time?

Last year my husband ¹(and)/ but I went on holiday to Bordeaux, in France. I don't like flying ²so / because we went by train. ³When / So we arrived in Bordeaux, we rented a car ⁴and / but drove to our hotel. We loved the hotel ⁵so / because it was very quiet. We both love walking ⁶so / because we went for a long walk every day. The food at the hotel was very good ⁷and / but it was easy to order ⁸so / because the menus were in English! We also went sightseeing in Bordeaux, ⁹so / but we didn't take any photos ¹⁰when / because I left the camera at the hotel! ¹¹When / So we left Bordeaux, we didn't want to go home. Maybe we can go back next year.

b Read about Kathy's holiday again. Choose the correct words.

6 a Think about your last holiday. Make notes in the table.

Which country / city did you go to?	
When did you go?	
Who did you go with?	
Where did you stay?	
How did you travel around?	
Where did you go and what did you do?	

b Write about your last holiday. Use your notes in **6a** and *because*, *so* and *when*.

Tick (✓) the things you can do in English in the Reading and Writing Progress Portfolio, p72.

Reading and Writing Portfolio 10

Reading greetings cards; a thank-you email
Writing messages on greetings cards; word order: review; a thank-you email
Review Present Simple; Past Simple; *be going to*

Happy birthday!

1 Match cards A–C to greetings 1–3.

A

B

C

1 To Diana
Good luck with your new job!
See you soon!
Love Frank and Rachel

2 To Diana
HAPPY BIRTHDAY!
Have a fantastic day!
Lots of love
Beth xx

3 To Diana and Eddie
Congratulations on your engagement!
Best wishes
Patrick

HELP WITH WRITING
Messages on greetings cards

2 Read these messages. Check new words in a dictionary.

Happy | birthday! / anniversary! / New Year!

Good luck with your | new job! / exams! / driving test!

Congratulations on your | engagement! / wedding! / new baby!

Have a great / fantastic day!
See you soon!
Love / Lots of love / Best wishes

TIP • We usually write *Love* or *Lots of love* for people we know very well. We usually write *Best wishes* for people we don't know very well.

3 Look at these messages. Fill in the gaps with these words.

~~To~~	Have
love	Happy
day	

¹ <del>To</del> Ray and Alice
² _____ anniversary!
³ _____ a great ⁴ _____ !
Lots of ⁵ _____
Georgina

| luck | your |
| To | wishes |

⁶ _____ Mariano
Good ⁷ _____ with ⁸ _____ exams!
Best ⁹ _____
Jill

| on | new |
| soon | Love |

To Cecilia and Marcus
Congratulations ¹⁰ _____ your
¹¹ _____ baby!
See you ¹² _____ !
¹³ _____
Fred, Wendy and family

HELP WITH WRITING Word order: review

4 a Look at these sentences. Notice the word order.

subject	verb	object
I	have	a car.
They	like	football.

b Look at this sentence. Extra words usually go before the verb (A) or at the end of the sentence (B).

A   B
↓   ↓
We play tennis .

A (before the verb)
- frequency adverbs (*always*, *usually*, *never*, etc.)
- *also*
- *both*

B (at the end of the sentence)
- phrases with *every* (*every day*, *every week*, etc.)
- extra information (*with a friend*, *in London*, etc.)
- *together*

TIP • With the verb *be*, we put frequency adverbs, *also*, *both*, etc. <u>after</u> the verb: *I'm always tired. It's also John's birthday. We're both doctors*, etc.

5 Read Diana's email to her friend Beth. Put the words in brackets ( ) in the correct place.

Dear Beth

Thank you very much for your birthday card and the present.
                                                every day
(every day →) It's a beautiful watch and I wear it ⋀ .

(on Saturday →) I had a very nice birthday. **(together →)**

I met my sister in town and we went shopping. **(also, in the**

evening →) I went to a concert with Eddie. **(both →)** The

concert was fantastic and we had a great time.

Life in London is very good. **(with a TV company →)** I have a

new job. **(never →)** I love the job, but I get home before 8 p.m.

(also →) Eddie is very busy. **(always, together →)** We're very

tired, but we're very happy. **(last month →)** Did you know that

we got engaged? **(next July →)** We're going to get married!

Lots of love Diana

---

6 Read Diana's email again. Answer these questions.

1 Who did Diana go shopping with?

2 What did Diana and Eddie do on Saturday evening?

3 When did Diana and Eddie get engaged?

4 When are they going to get married?

7 a Imagine it was your birthday last weekend. You are going to write a thank-you email to a friend. Make notes in the table.

What did your friend give you?	
What did you do on your birthday?	
What do you do in the week?	
What did you do last month?	
What are your future plans?	

b Write your thank-you email. Use your notes from **7a**. Check the word order.

Tick (✓) the things you can do in English in the Reading and Writing Progress Portfolio, p72.

Starter Reading and Writing Progress Portfolio

Tick the things you can do in English.

Portfolio	Reading	Writing
1 p52	☐ I can understand simple conversations.	☐ I can use full stops and question marks. ☐ I can use capital letters at the beginning of a sentence, and for *I*, countries, cities and names.
2 p54	☐ I can understand information about people on business cards. ☐ I can understand a simple form.	☐ I can use capital letters for titles, addresses, postcodes, companies and nationalities. ☐ I can fill in a form with my personal information (name, address, etc.).
3 p56	☐ I can understand a simple holiday email.	☐ I can use apostrophes. ☐ I can write sentences with *and* and *but*. ☐ I can write a simple holiday email.
4 p58	☐ I can understand a simple internet profile.	☐ I can write simple sentences with the correct word order. ☐ I can write an internet profile about myself.
5 p60	☐ I can understand information about people (age, family, job, free time activities, etc.).	☐ I can write sentences with *because* and *also*. ☐ I can write about a person I know.
6 p62	☐ I can understand simple tourist information (things to do, when places open and close, etc.) in a newspaper.	☐ I can write about places that tourists go to in my town or city.
7 p64	☐ I can understand information about things that people love, like and hate.	☐ I can write sentences with *and*, *but* and object pronouns. ☐ I can use *both* and *together* in sentences. ☐ I can write about myself and a person in my family.
8 p66	☐ I can find information in adverts for films, plays, concerts (place, time, etc.). ☐ I can understand a simple email about last weekend.	☐ I can use *a / an* and *the* in simple sentences and phrases. ☐ I can write a simple description of a film, play or concert.
9 p68	☐ I can understand a simple description of a holiday.	☐ I can use *because*, *so* and *when* in sentences. ☐ I can describe a holiday.
10 p70	☐ I can understand simple messages from friends or family. ☐ I can understand a simple thank-you email.	☐ I can write a greetings card (a birthday card, a good luck card, etc.). ☐ I can write a simple thank-you email to a friend.